HÏJĀB

Unveiling Queer Muslim Lives

Hijab: Unveiling Queer Muslim Lives is a groundbreaking anthology of queer Muslim stories. This book represents a set of voices from various backgrounds and generations whose stories are true... In almost all of these pieces one sees the difficulties queer Muslims journey through in order to reconcile their sexuality with their spirituality.

Any compassionate human being would be deeply moved by the way that truth and individuality is embraced in every single story. It is thought-provoking and often heartbreaking... *Hijab* should be required reading for every parent, teacher, religious leader and politician as it shows all of us how important it is that we be more attentive, tolerant and accepting to aspects of difference in religion, race, ethnicity and sexuality.

I highly recommend this selection of heart-rending stories to anyone with a personal interest – or quite simply, to anyone who cares.
– *Mariam Ismail-Baderoon (Educationist)*

For many years I've heard stories of young gay Muslims in Cape Town and abroad who've taken their own lives because they felt helpless in the face of societal beliefs that dictate they simply could not be Muslim and gay at the same time. These sad stories made it clear to me that action is needed – and if this anthology saves even one life, then every person who contributed to this book should hold their heads high.
– *Sieraaj Ahmed (Journalist)*

This initiative to provide a social history of the lives of queer Muslims is an outstanding venture. I recommend that everyone should read this book. It provides the space for people to do some introspection and look at their own values and beliefs. We need to engage!
– *Riedwaan Jacobs (New Media Manager, Good Hope FM)*

We often hear about people having challenges about their sexuality, especially if they are gay. It is often difficult for people to access supportive people or resources to assist them in their plight, especially in the rural areas. This book provides a reflection of some of these complex issues. Although it mainly reflects on Muslim lives, the dynamics are universal in its approach and can widely benefit people across the globe. It could also strengthen other gay individuals to assert themselves as proudly gay citizens. In 1994 South Africa legislated one of the most liberating constitutions in the world. Let's use it!
– *Fatima Shabodien (Director of Women on Farms)*

This anthology goes a long way to providing the much-needed dais for a minority grouping that for too long has been denied a right to be heard. It explores, in a very real manner, the challenges faced by ordinary folk trying assiduously to be accepted by a society that is often brutal and cruel.
– *Rafiek Mammon, Editor and Playwright*

HÏJĀB

Unveiling Queer Muslim Lives

Edited by Pepe Hendricks

THE INNER CIRCLE

Published in 2009
by The Inner Circle
P.O. Box 18107
Wynberg
7824
Cape Town
South Africa

www.theinnercircle.org.za

© 2009 The Inner Circle

ISBN 978-1-920355-20-3

Editor: Pepe Hendricks
Cover image: Nazeem Hendricks
Production: COMPRESS.dsl

Distributed by African Minds
4 Eccleston Place
Somerset West
South Africa
7130
www.africanminds.co.za

Contents

	Foreword	vii
	Introduction	ix
	Gay people are people like anyone else	xii
1.	A confused state	1
2.	Fair share of life	6
3.	A lonely soul	14
4.	Somalian in need	21
5.	Living amongst the Queer	31
6.	A secret well kept	38
7.	Brothers	44
8.	A road less travelled	54
9.	Mistaken identity	58
10.	Finding love	65
11.	Trials in love	71
12.	This is reality	83
13.	Queer reflection	91
14.	Happiness	99
15.	Daddy's boy	108
16.	New beginnings	118
17.	The dreaded flight	129
18.	So far, so good	140
19.	Lost	152
20.	Cut off, but okay	162
21.	Two heads, one tale	172
22.	Coming out	194
	Glossary	201
	More about The Inner Circle	207

Foreword

Once again we thank our Creator for the guidance, inspiration and courage He has given us in order to bring this project to fruition. It has indeed taken an enormous amount of time, effort and patience from all those who have been instrumental in putting this book together.

We also pray that our Creator guides the reader of this book to an understanding and appreciation of the stories told by Islam's most unlikely story-tellers.

I have always felt a deep sense of obligation to the struggle of queer Muslims. Is it a good Muslim practice to disregard someone who is different from the mainstream simply because they are not fitting in with our interpretation of Islam? Is it just to brand anyone an apostate (*murtad*) when they are still an ardent believer and practicing Muslim? How dare we judge as mere mortals when the lives of every single person in this book have been tarnished by the residing judgement of our society?

More and more people are acknowledging that Islam does not allow people to make judgements. Siti Musdah Mulia of the Indonesia Conference of Religions and Peace said that homosexuality was from God and should be considered natural and that it was not pushed only by passion. According to the *Jakarta Post* she cited the Quran, Al-Hujurat (49:13) as bearing testimony to that.

> ... one of the blessings for human beings was that all men and women are equal, regardless of ethnicity, wealth, social positions or even sexual orientation. 'There is no difference

between lesbians and nonlesbians. In the eyes of God, people are valued based on their piety...'

'And talking about piety [it] is God's prerogative to judge,' she added. 'The essence of the religion (Islam) is to humanise humans, respect and dignify them.'

I want to thank my brother Nazeem Hendricks for his time, willingness and creativity in painting the picture for the cover of this book; a painting that reflects the double lives most of us live for fear of being rejected.

I also want to thank Pepe Hendricks who has made unlimited sacrifices to edit this book: a truly spirited individual guided by his compassion for his fellow human beings, his obsession with justice and his passion for Islam.

This book would not have been possible without the help of the dedicated TIC staff and passionate individuals such as Qiyaam Jantjies, Branden Grant, Mariam Ismail-Baderoon, Zuraida Dramat, Zaid Noordien, Zahra Hendricks, Angus Botha, Verenia Keet, Gypsy and all those who helped in various ways to complete the book.

Last but not least, a special thank you to our funders:

- Echoing Green, who gave support and seed funding to The Inner Circle.
- Atlantic Philanthropies without whom this book would have only been an idea.
- The Ford Foundation, for having had faith in our work and funded our Public Education and Training.
- Astraea Lesbian Foundation, for having funded our projects for the last three years.

God bless you all as you journey with us unveiling the lives of queer Muslims.

Imam Muhsin Hendricks
Founder and Director of the TIC

Introduction

Hijab: Unveiling Queer Muslim Lives is the first known collection of South African Muslim stories of queer individuals. *Hijab* is the Arabic word meaning to cover, to veil, or to shelter. In further definition it is metaphysical, where *al-hijab* refers to the veil, which separates people or the world from Allah. This anthology of stories seeks to reflect personal life stories relating to Islam and sexual diversity, especially of Muslims who are queer. The word queer is often regarded as offensive and derisive, but many LGBTI people have reclaimed and re-appropriated it to describe a sexual orientation and/or gender identity or gender expression that does not conform to heteronormative society.

This book aims to make people realise that it is possible to be both Muslim and queer. It shares stories of people that have struggled to reconcile their spirituality and their sexuality. There are also stories that illustrate the oneness of being, and reflections on how a lack of knowledge around queer issues leads to condemnation of many homosexuals. Although it predominantly focuses on Muslim stories, it is universal in its approach in dealing with spirituality, rather than religion.

The stories are records of authentic stories which have been edited into a narrative form that maintains a story-telling method. The Inner Circle has decided to keep the identities of people anonymous so as to protect the individual's privacy. Hence the names of authors are not mentioned. Characters are also provided with fictitious names. Some stories were recorded and transcribed by TIC staff members and volunteers, for people who preferred not to write it themselves. Due to the editing process some information may be slightly distorted, but the stories are as authentic as possible.

Hopefully the stories will touch you as much as they did the people involved in the documentation and recording processes. There are various emotional reflections, such as humanity, inspiration, generosity, authenticity, faith, Allah-consciousness, caring, humour, friendship, love, courage and sharing. They also reflect how Muslims had to overcome adversity in their struggles and experiences of personal growth. Some stories are unique, unusual, funny and interesting.

Queer people are often taught to believe that homosexuality is wrong. Through socialisation they learn to feel unacceptable, 'bad', worthless. They find themselves at the mercy of the horrified gaze of mainstream society who they can't trust, but need to defend themselves from. In order to break this state of being all individuals need to start by thinking differently.

In dealing with our state of being it is a good idea to look at our development from a psycho-spiritual perspective – we need to find the Creation within. In so doing, we will enable greater self-esteem and resilience in dealing with discrimination. Indeed, a direct relationship with the Creator is always fundamental in Islam and guides the personal understanding or resolution that can be reached.

Three areas for the individual to consider in thinking differently are:

- The realisation that self-esteem is not dependent on others, but rather the self. Hence people who are queer may need to interdependently develop their own sense of self as 'good'. Often help is needed in this regard as the individual may be clouded with the teachings of orthodox society and cannot use an *ijtihadic* (independent reasoning) approach to determine their well-being.
- Finding and connecting with one's perfection, one's SPIRIT!
- Turning to the right place.

As you read the journey of others, may it guide your path and may you find your inner light!

We also invite readers to share their comments, concerns and challenges after reading this anthology of short stories.

Pepe Hendricks
Editor

Gay people are people like anyone else

If a gay man has a profound connection to his faith, deep knowledge, and a way with words and rhetoric that can inspire me to be a better Muslim, then of course I would be delighted to listen to his sermon and to pray behind him. Orientation has nothing to do with the matter.

Most Muslims believe that homosexual acts are a sin. Many believe that simply the fact of being gay is a sin. I disagree. The Quran, like the Bible, has passages about the people of Sodom. Two things are apparent from the story. First, it is a story of intended rape – the men who come forth from Sodom intended to have their way with Lot's guests regardless of whether they wanted to or not.

But more than that, it is a story of a town where orientation has been turned on its head. Men who are naturally heterosexual have abandoned their wives in favour of fulfilling their desires with men.

– *Imam Pamela Taylor, speaking at the TIC Annual International Retreat (24–27 April 2009) in Cape Town.*

Imam Pamela Taylor, from Ohio USA, is co-founder of Muslims for Progressive Values and director of the Islamic Writers Alliance. She is a member of the national board of advisors to the Network of Spiritual Progressives, and served as co-chair of the Progressive Muslim Union for two years. She is a strong supporter of the Woman Imam Movement, which seeks the full participation of Muslim women in every aspect of life, including the pulpit.

1

A confused state

It was a rainy Friday afternoon when I first brought him home. I had spent lots of time at his place and I thought that it was high time that I returned his generosity. I could feel the eminent dangers and fears that it evoked within me, but I knew that I just had to do it. I thought that I would never be able to live through the actual act of doing this but, on the other hand, it just had to be done.

I can still hear the penetrating razor sharp shrill in the voice of my mother's husband, 'What the bloody hell? He's got the audacity to bring that *moffie* into my house and nogal a *kaffer* on top of it.' The immediate response of my defensive mother was filled with a sense of pain and fear. 'Maanie, leave the boy alone; he will grow up into a decent man, one day. Maybe even better than you!'

Her favourite words were 'live above it'. She would never let anything deter her; she would be above any situation no matter how bad. That's how I felt at that moment in time. I was not going to allow him to upset me. I would 'live above it' and not let it affect me. Although she was so strong in coping with any disastrous situation it seemed a pity that she could not be strong enough to confront him – better still leave him. My mother's pathetic attempt of an existence sometimes drove me mad. Her life was fixed in rearing me and keeping house. That's all! Oh yes, she did some sewing for the neighbours when he wasn't around. (He must never know!) Fortunately the baby boom did not affect her, as I was the only child. After me she was too scared to have any more. In fact, he was unable to have children of his own; this could possibly have been the reason for his mean streak.

My family had moved around tons of times and meeting a true friend was extremely difficult. Every time I became close to someone, it was time to move on to a new destination.

I only knew Achmat for ten months. He was the only real friend I ever had. We were like true brothers. He was closer to me than anyone else in the entire world. He was never judgemental. It was to him that I turned in times of hardship and pain. He would never ostracise me. He was a person that I could confide in.

We spent the whole afternoon behind the closed door of the bedroom. There was grumbling in the kitchen and while working in the room, I could hear the voices growing louder and louder. The words were all a jumble to my ears because at times like those I switched off automatically. What provoked the raucous babble was entirely my fault. I should not have brought him home. I was a bad boy. I am a wicked child. I knew that there would be no sleep for me that night. I could hear in the tone of the voices that it would carry on throughout the night.

It was time for Achmat to go home. The best way to go was through the side door to avoid any further embarrassment or conflict. I looked at him as he walked down the driveway. He was bigger built and better looking than I was. He really was my hero, the greatest role model in my life – my inspiration. Maybe even, maybe… no, it could not have been. I so wished I was him or maybe even that I was a bigger part of his life. I wished that I could hide myself in his big beautiful body. I wondered to myself if he would still be my friend after he knew. If he really knew the true me, the evil monster that I was, he would not want to be a part of my life. I always did the 'wrong' things. I was the one who always caused it. I always needed to be punished. I so wished I could be like him. I watched him go, until he was long out of sight. I wondered if he would denounce me if he knew. Would he still be my friend? I suddenly became afraid of who I was.

It was almost like *deja vu*, except that some scenes in life are repeated so often that we never know the differences between past, future and present. It all becomes the same after a while. I had to prepare myself for a night of safety. It was only six o'clock and the sun was setting. A gorgeous crimson sky reflected on our house. It was a beautiful scene, but I had to get ready for the danger that grew in the womb of a house ready to rupture. I made sure that the window was opened, ready for take-off. I packed a little overnight bag and placed it underneath my bed. I bathed myself and got ready for dinner. We normally ate at seven o'clock, but I knew that tonight my mom would bring my food to the bedroom. I had to remain in the bedroom to avoid any further conflict – as if that was possible. This is how it always began. It was always my fault.

When my mom brought my dinner, she had the face of a sixty-year-old and she was only forty. I looked at her and I could see the rapid aging process of a few minutes that took place within her. It was always the case. There were days when she would become aged and ugly within a short space of time. I thought to myself, 'Why do you always have to look for trouble? Why do you always have to say things to upset him? You are also to blame. Why do you provoke him? Don't challenge him! He is your husband!' But it was not my fault; it was he that aged her so much. No, it was me. I am the stirrer of trouble. I always caused it. Her face was pale as she mumbled to me, 'Eat quickly I need to clean the dishes.' By this time the tomb grew to a slight, very slight din. One could sense that this was the calm before the storm.

At midnight I slept in a state of semi-awareness, listening to the voices of the house growing louder and louder. It was him, this figure of a publicly orthodox Muslim role model – he was sitting 'in hiding' with his glass of whiskey. I awaited the crescendo, which was usually my cue for escape.

Then a door slams. There is a hysterical screech as if a woman is maimed, or raped. I am too scared to move. I know what's happening, I don't have to guess. It's my fault. I will have to pay the price. But why her, oh Lord? Why her? She did nothing. 'Leave her alone you bastard,' I keep saying to myself. Without warning the door is flung open, but I am prepared. He storms in, armed with the belt of reckoning. This will allow me to repay my deed of ill doing. He shouts out his wrath and condemnation. 'You always cause it. You are a wicked monster!' he curses. I allow him to punish me by putting the belt through my face. It is the first course of cleansing and healing, and for him to get his satisfaction. Then I am in flight. I grab my emergency kit and fly through the window. He is too big and clumsy to follow me through the window. So I am safe. For how long I do not know.

I hope that he has had his satisfaction, so that he will not be looking for me. After a sprint around the block of houses, I return to the house. In the yard there is an enormous square slab almost the size of a single bed, just slightly higher. It is the slab my mother does the washing on. As I lie on the cold cement slab, I say to myself, 'One day you will pay. Every dog has his day and you will pay.' The stone is my witness, my refuge that will keep me alert and not allow me to sink into a deep sleep. I cannot allow myself to become too comfortable. I cannot sleep because it would be too dangerous. I lie there in semi-consciousness, waiting for the new dawn. Justice has prevailed. I have served my sentence today for looking at a beautiful boy. The punishment is lodged in this stone of reflection.

I have often thought of how wonderful life could be after my sentence is over. But it will never end. I am always doing the wrong thing. I always need punishment. I must always be alone. Because I am useless. This must be more than the hundredth time that I have spent on this slab. 'Is this what it feels like to be dead? Is this what happens to all of us?'

Suddenly a chill runs through me. A reflection of the past comes to me. I no longer feel safe on the rock.

The last time he found my secret place he punished me even more. That was the first night of the belt. It came so fast and unexpected. After the first time, there was *his* belt that thrust itself in a different way. The night of blood. The recurrence. The perpetuating nightmares that even followed me into my bedroom as I lay alone. My mind was in a state of rage and panic. He found me. Yes, this Allah-conscious hypocrite. This community-loving fraud. He raped me! It was terrible. But, I behaved badly. It was long ago, I forget… I forget what happened next. Just a mumble of *Allah Hu Akbar* on my lips. I was barely able to utter the words. Trying to recapture the nightmare. The night of blood. *Allah Hu Akbar*! Heal my body and pain! *Allah Hu Akbar*! Oh, hear my cry! Take away the marks of the beast! The displaced memories of the past.

The sun greets me with a warm smile. The tinted sky is the sign that a new day has arrived. The splendour of the morning's rays fills my soul with a new life, a new beginning for a new day. As the whole neighbourhood lies asleep, I am the only one to greet the sun. It is as if yesterday never happened. But yesterday will still be today, yesterday will be tomorrow and yesterday will remain forever. My sticky body will bear testimony on the Day of Judgement. It wasn't my fault! It was never me!

It took years for me to realise that it is okay to be gay.

2

Fair share of life

Those were the days, a simple thought running through my head as I look back on my life. I sit and smile as I reflect. I believe that Salt River was a wonderful place to start out my humble life. Of course, it had its challenges…

I think of the time when I was in primary school. I chuckle as I think of all those bullies. They always thought that I was a weakling, someone they could knock about and take advantage of. Little did they know that interfering with me was a serious mistake. I could always rely on my twin brother for aid in this time of difficulty. He defended me on many occasions. Yes, I was often the target for abuse and jeering of the boys in our home-town and my brother was the strong one, the protector. We were a group of seven healthy brothers. My mother yearned for a daughter, but unfortunately couldn't have one. I unknowingly assumed the role of being my mother's daughter – perhaps not only to make my mother happy but also because of sexuality being inherent at birth. So I guess I cannot really say that it was only because of my mother.

During my first year at school, my teacher informed my mother that I was truly artistic and that she should pay special attention to me. She was trying to encourage my mom to nurture that special, talented side of me. I remember the grin on my mother's face, much like some women do when they're in doubt. I wasn't sure whether she fully understood what my teacher had relayed to her. *Did she mean artistic or autistic?* For a while she thought that I was indeed autistic and was very protective of me. My family still have a good laugh when they affectionately speak of my mother's sweet naiveté.

I felt comfortable around the girls at school, especially since they were more accepting of me. I felt a certain kinship with them that I didn't have with boys. I liked what they liked and I felt comfortable sharing things with them. When I was thirteen I told my mother that I would have my own flat or house one day. She merely smiled her sweet noncommittal smile and said, *'Yes son, you will one day have a pleasant little place of your own with a beautiful wife and family.'* If she knew... If she only *knew!*

She always thought that I was a big dreamer. In our family and in the rest of the neighbourhood there were loads of people who never reached their dreams. I don't think there were many who had dreams. They lacked direction – lacked a zest for life you could say. Even now they are all grown-up, married and happy to be right there – still living with their parents. Everyone always said they would leave, but none of them did. So her laughter was justified, I guess.

During my high school days the level of bullying increased. I was constantly subjected to their surges of testosterone and was more of a target than ever before. I attended a school that was outside of my immediate environment. To crown it all it was a boys' school, Spes Bona Senior Secondary. The school was held in high esteem. Pupils from various rural towns flocked to the school because of its excellent academic record. There were always snide comments from the broader community that implied that this was an elite school. They also said that the boys who attended the school were all *moffies*. Inside the school, it was a different story. In fact, some of the boys were extremely macho. I clearly remember how the boys mocked me for being a wee bit effeminate. I was always dressed in a different way even though I wore the prescribed school uniform. I was impeccably stylish and wore it with grace. Outside of school, I had a mixed dress code, but always neat. I carried myself like a model.

Like anyone else would, I resented the callous and vicious verbal assaults and sometimes minor incidents of physical abuse that was thrust my way. This was hurtful at the time. I felt so humiliated. Yes I was different to the majority of the boys at the school, but I had a right to be who I was meant to be. I was unique! I was different! At that time the constitution of the country was not in my favour.

As my poor self-image started to crumble, I met Nazeem. He changed the negative belief I started to develop. He was one of the soccer players at school. He was a strong, brave boy and he was handsome too. He was more than your average good-looking TV star. He was deep! He knew all about life and also knew how to explore life and live it to the full. He brought me out of my shell. Like most of my peers at the time, he too had a 'girlfriend'. This new friend I made was instrumental in allowing me to accept myself for who I am, regardless of what the mainstream community said.

I remember the bravery of this boy. One day out of the blue, he publicly kissed me outside the school ground. It was my first real kiss. It was clean and based on friendship but it was one that gave me confidence and acceptance. It brought excitement to my life. I remember it as if it were yesterday. I felt so lost in that sweet kiss. The affection that oozed through my body told me that which I so long denied. I couldn't imagine how anyone could not want to be like this. I longed for him after that. I remember wanting him to take the friendship further, to another level; unfortunately that was never meant to be. He chose to have a girlfriend, so that is as far as it went. He was only experimenting whilst I was ready to develop a deeper relationship. I wanted more of him, more from him. Alas, we parted swiftly without a glimmer of our friendship remaining. This was not deliberate because two months after our friendship, his family moved to another place. There were no regrets. In fact, it was a life-changing experience that made me feel good about myself. It also showed me who I was and who I was going to become.

During my adolescent years my family moved to a rather

conservative neighbourhood on the Cape Flats where the majority of people were Muslim. It was a part of Athlone called Surrey Estate. This was closer to where most of our relatives lived. I didn't really know them all that well. I was pleasantly surprised to find out that one of my cousins was just like me. We developed an extremely strong bond. Like they say, birds of a feather…

We could provide each other with the space to just be ourselves. He would come around more and more often, and we would spend an immeasurable amount of time together. He was attractive, large and quite forceful, which were characteristics and features he developed through playing rugby. He also developed an immense amount of tension because of the duality between his sexual orientation and his much loved game. I still remember the wonderful moments we spent together as teenagers exploring our sexuality. He was indeed a very sensual and intense being. Every moment with him was a moment of joy even though it was only temporary. He fulfilled me. Together we could come to terms with ourselves and the rest of the world. We could be completely whole. I really knew him. This was a memorable time to say the least.

When I turned seventeen I ran away from home and stayed in a hostel in the city. After about a month my twin brother came looking for me and took me home. I sometimes think of all the sleepless nights my mother must have endured.

I left school at an early age, as I wanted to explore and exploit my sexuality for what it was. I befriended an older guy and as things progressed we moved in together. I felt rather excited as I was realising one of my dreams. We had some really happy moments. I got myself a job at Irvin and Johnson and I finally became that independent person I was yearning to be.

At the age of twenty I decided that I had had enough of working for a minimum wage. I started looking for better work prospects and approached Groote Schuur Hospital where I started as a general worker. I would spend my nights studying in an attempt to complete my schooling which I had irresponsibly neglected. After completing my studies I decided to devote all my energy to giving my utmost performance at work.

Even though I was born into Islam, I found it extremely difficult to reconcile my faith with my sexual identity. This was cause for tremendous confusion. To make some sense of my life I decided to abstain from sex all together. It was at this juncture that I became obsessed with religious order. Hence I joined the Catholic Church at St Mary's Cathedral in Cape Town where I was baptised. I received my first holy communion on the same day that I was confirmed. I then hid away at a monastery and hoped that they would train me in mission work or to help people in some way. But all they gave me to do were little jobs working in the garden, doing the washing and ironing, never anything that I felt was spiritually fulfilling. I spent about six months there. I was away from the rest of the world to seek solitude and the opportunity to reinvent myself. I felt that I was a bit lost after converting to Christianity and I wanted to strengthen my bond with God. I wanted to find the place within myself that felt completely whole and right. My feelings were all over the place and I wasn't sure what to do next. I left the monastery and got my job back at Groote Schuur Hospital. They knew that I was a faithful and dedicated worker.

During my first few weeks back, one of the staff doctors recommended that I go to the Avalon Psychiatric Unit for therapy. This was an educational experience and I found that not all psychiatrists are bad. It really worked for me. I found guidance, the answers I needed, and much more. I stayed there for a period of three months. I was a bit weary of the medication that they might have given, so I was very relieved when they informed me that I would not be using any.

After this episode of my life, I went back to live with my mom. At this point, the family came together and it was decided that I should go to Mecca, in Saudi Arabia. They believed that if I saw the holy land, then I would gain a different perspective on life.

Mecca offered a buzz of excitement as there were various people doing amazing things. I was interested in so much that I didn't know where to start. The buildings and the history behind it all was truly breathtaking. I was especially surprised to see how casual the men were about sex. I was walking past a toilet in Mecca where there were many men standing around. I noticed that they would look at each other with a strange kind of a look. I never experienced this before, but somehow I sensed a lust-filled energy in their gazes. There was a connection in those eyes and there were words running through that connection. I stood watching for a while and noticed that they would signal each other and then enter the toilets together. About half an hour later, they came out separately with smug looks on their faces. They had a look of satisfaction. I had a culture shock, men in Mecca were yearning for other men and engaging with their feelings. Men were having sex with other men everywhere. It wasn't merely a local thing; it was universal. Anyway, my three week stay in Mecca was truly memorable because of these new insights that I had gained. I loathed the despicable behaviour that I saw in the men's toilets in Mecca. Mecca of all places! However, I immediately felt revitalised and I was able to build a truly loving connection to my old religion, Islam. I didn't like this kind of approach as I preferred to have an intimate and one-on-one relationship.

After the experience in Mecca I found that there was hope to remain Muslim and gay at the same time. Now all I hoped to find was that other person that would make me happy. Somehow I always attracted negative people into my life. By negative I mean people who seemed to be right for me, but were not. The ones that I believe I could grow with, but could not. However, I would later realise that I was totally wrong about them. *Was it them, or was it me?*

On my return to Cape Town I met a lovely Catholic coloured guy named Marcellino who happened to be just the right aphrodisiac to restart my life. We started dating and soon decided to move in together. To my surprise, I found it quite entertaining that my mother got on so well with Marcellino. She actually knew that we were in an intimate relationship and she accepted it. We were happy together in a wooden structure at the back of my mother's house, and we were content to live this way for a while. When I turned twenty-three, I bought my first house in Rocklands, Mitchell's Plain. In our new house we became bored with our routine lifestyle and decided to spice things up by exploring different sexual practices. This was the beginning of the end of our relationship. I had to put a stop to it as I didn't want sexual deviance to become the basis of our relationship. Hence Marcellino was no more.

I needed a fresh start. The house left too many memories, so I sold it and moved to Pelican Heights. As fate would have it my new home was next to a mosque. This was coincidental because my life in Rocklands had become very wayward. I even denounced Islam and embraced Catholicism. I clearly remember crying, very emotionally, every time I heard the *athaan*, the call to prayer. It soon became too much for me to cope with. I was spending most of my time crying like a baby. Eventually I approached the imam of the mosque who happened to know my mother extremely well. With his intervention, he approached the community elders and insisted that I revert to Islam. I had to recite the *kalimah shahadah*, a prayer which is used as a declaration of devotion to Allah. It is with these words that I renewed my vows to Islam before witnesses in the mosque. Ever since then I've decided to live as a Muslim, and even though I still like hearing the hymns of the church and still enjoy attending church I want to live and die a Muslim. I felt that I shouldn't exclude friends or associates from my life no matter what their faith was because even the Prophet Muhammad (peace be upon him) reached out to people of various religions. I suppose that's the reason I have a soft spot for all forms of organised faiths.

I've always had a passion for antiques, art and all things

beautiful and this motivated me to open an antique shop. I bought a two bedroom house in Observatory from where I traded. I had the shop for a period of two years but I found it financially impossible to be in two places at the same time, with my loyalty always to the medical fraternity. I had to close the shop. Perhaps when I retire I'll reopen and venture into a mixture of modern and antique pieces since I absolutely love spending time at auctions.

I've met some very interesting people on my journey through life. I guess if I had to evaluate my weak points then one of them would be that I lack faith in people because I always end up being hurt by them. This is perhaps an area for me to improve on and maybe better myself in. Another would be to finish all those unfinished projects.

I'm hopeful for an improvement in my life. Since I've attended various activities of The Inner Circle there has been a conscious shift in my thinking as well as in the way that I relate to the broader community. I no longer have to carry that heavy load that's been weighing me down. I'm finding it rather easy to engage on matters of spirituality and gender. For some obscure reason I thought that this kind of engagement was exclusively available to the *ulema*. I feel stronger now than I've ever been before and I'm eternally grateful to the The Inner Circle team.

I'm forty-three now and find myself single yet again. I am hopeful that I will attract the right kind of people who will sustain and will help to enhance my life. After all, I have a meaningful contribution to make to this world. I've reached an interesting period in my life where I'm pretty comfortable in my own space. Some of my close friends tell me that I'm too goal driven but I just smile knowing in my heart that one has to be fully devoted to your goals. I sometimes wonder whether I have neglected my social life but I am comforted by the knowledge that I have played my part in the roller-coaster ride of life.

My advice for the youth of today is: be patient with yourself and the world will be your oyster.

3

A lonely soul

I was always a free spirit! Even before I was born there was a yearning to express myself and move about. I started crawling, walking, talking and running before the average age. Nothing could keep me back. No one could understand it but me. Even during the gestation period, I longed to be free from the confines of the womb that bore me. I was born only seven months into the pregnancy. I am told that from the instant that I was born, I loved this new world and I wanted to explore it as soon as possible. There were scents, sounds and fun things to do, and I needed to try them all. This mindset, made me very independent, which was just as well. This taught me to stand my ground against those that wanted to rob me of my freedom. Yes, the bullies of this world always wanted to get a piece of me. I made peace with the fact that this world was not as nice as I once thought it would be, but I continued to press on.

During primary school, I went through the motions of life, without really trying to stand out, but this didn't work for me because I wanted to be tall. I wanted to make my mark, to be known and to be proud of my accomplishments. I accepted every grace I received and felt that if this was what life was all about, then I have to do something to make it better. When I told my teacher this, she just laughed. Then I enquired as to why she was laughing at me, and then she just shook her head and told me to do a drawing of a horse. Today I hate horses, drawing and drawings!

My wise mother, realising at an early stage that I was a special, or rather a very different child, encouraged me to wear a *ta'weez* at all times to keep all things evil and unjust away from me. This was encouraged by our local imam. I merely thought that he agreed to it because she was a very persuasive person. From then on, my childhood was a happy one. There were the normal, everyday little conflicts that affected me as with all children growing up, but besides that, I was a relatively happy little child, living a very lonely life.

Four years after attending *madressa*, at the age of about twelve, I started mingling more with other children and developing friendships with them. I remember the first day I met Shuaib as if it was still today, maybe just a few hours ago. Yes, he was my first real friend that I discovered at *madressa*. He was about the same age as I was, maybe a bit older by months. We bonded instantaneously and a friendship arose. It blossomed easily as we did everything at *madressa* together. The connection that developed was filled and inspired by a strong, spiritual connection. We would not only spend time together at *madressa*, but were soon getting together on other occasions like public holidays. I watched our connection grow stronger and stronger as we spent more and more time together. I sat myself down and tried thinking of what he meant to me. He was many things: he was a protector, my brother in Islam and my closest friend. It was a beautiful journey for me personally, and I would have liked to believe that we were an unbeatable team. I thought we were going to be friends forever, but the universe had other plans for us, and we soon parted as young adults. Shuaib got married and I was left to figure out where I fit into the greater scheme of things. I had a fantasy of saving myself for the one I love, so even though he wanted our relationship to go to a sexual level, I never allowed it to.

I started working for a manufacturing company in Ottery, which dealt with furniture. I liked this business and could see myself staying in this business for most of my life. I had dreams of growing in this business and I started throwing myself into it. I gave my work my all and left my love life behind me as I tried to get as involved in the business as I could.

This might have been part of the cause for the great drama that was about to unfold in my life. It all started with minor things: I was shopping excessively, spending more than I could afford, I was running around the streets naked, I was just... being completely excessive, in a fanatical way. The time that it became clear to me was at work. I went to work as usual, had my coffee and was sitting at my desk. I sat there looking at worksheets and then I started talking to myself and then started ranting and raving. I went out into the open offices and started ranting about unnecessary things like why do we work, and for the pay we get. Why would anyone want to come to work and dress like this? Is this a fashion show? I completely lost track of what I was saying and doing, and soon my colleagues realised that something was seriously wrong. They quickly called my best friend at the time, and he said that I was fine when I was at his place that morning. They insisted that something was wrong with me, and this made my friend worried enough to come and see what was wrong with me. I was so lost; I didn't even feel ashamed of anything that I said or did. My friend tried to calm me down, but I shoved him away as if he were just another stranger to me. He then decided to call the police and when they arrived, they took me to Lentegeur Hospital for a mental assessment.

I was there for a while and they had placed me in a room full of people who were staring off into the distance and speaking to people who weren't there. I spent most of my days watching these people do all sorts of weird things and I'd wonder what I was doing here. One day, I just decided I had had enough and I ran away from the hospital. It wasn't easy, but I found a way, and even to this day, I cannot tell you how I escaped but just that I finally did. I ran from there straight to my old house where I had hidden a key, but in a few short hours, I was found again by the police. They arrested me and took me back to Lentegeur, where after a few episodes, they decided to move me again. I was moved around a lot during that time and found myself spending a full six months in Valkenberg Hospital for rehabilitation. I could not believe it when they diagnosed me as having a bipolar disorder. I did not know what it was and the doctor explained to me, in a very sincere way: 'The latest theory, although nothing is certain, is that bipolar disorder is caused by a chemical imbalance in the brain. It is incurable, but there is medication for you that helps keep it under control and you can therefore live a normal, unaffected life, as long as you keep taking your medication.'

I then vowed that I would live my life as best I could, and would take this medication and make the most of this life. I learnt to accept my condition and slipped into the routine of taking my medication easily.

Up until now, I had found no reason to tell my family that I was gay, but after finding out about my illness, I did not wish anything to keep me back or to make me feel as if I needed to worry about it. I needed to make sure nothing was going to affect me negatively and I didn't want to have to carry that burden of hiding while I needed to worry about my disorder.

I went home and found my mom at home. I told her I needed her to be there tonight when my dad came home, because I needed to discuss something with them. She looked at me as if to ask 'Something worse than being bipolar?'

I ignored this and waited for my dad to come home. I sat in my room readying myself for anything that might come my way. I didn't worry about it or anything because I knew it needed to be done and whatever the consequences thereof, they would have to come. I heard my father enter and I gave him time to settle down. Suppertime came and I went to have supper with them. As we finished, I did the dishes and then called them both to the dining-room, where I sat them down.

'I need to tell you something,' I said, and they wanted to butt in, but I stopped them. 'This is something important to me, and I need to tell it to you because it has been eating at me. The fact that I need to hide it from you makes me uncomfortable and makes me really worry about when you'll find out, and what you're going to say when you do. So here I am, finally ready to say it out loud, and I hope that you will accept it and you'll love me, regardless… I'm gay.'

The room was silent and I let that silence expand as I waited for their reply. I hoped that they would respond soon, but we sat there for a few minutes, until my mom broke it.

'How do you know?' she asked, hesitantly. She seemed very kind in her question, but I knew she was assessing me. I looked at her for a moment and thought of how to reply.

'I like being with guys,' I replied. 'I don't feel any attraction towards girls.'

'Oh,' was all she said and I accepted that. This she usually said if she couldn't argue a point. My father on the other hand just sat there without making a comment. Later, I found out that he believed I was going through a phase. Up until today, even living in the same house, he still hasn't come to terms with the fact that I'm gay. He still hopes that I'll eventually end up with a girl. He doesn't really speak to me any more, he just acknowledges my presence. It seems like he's trying to ignore that part of me, while trying to maintain his relationship with me.

I decided that as soon as I found a job, I would move out into a place of my own. When I moved on my own, the independence felt amazing, but the loneliness of not having anyone to share it with was excruciating. I was only in my mid-twenties, and I felt alone. I yearned for someone that I could share it with and who could cater to my every desire. I longed to find the man that was meant for me, and at this young age, this longing only grew.

I spent two years finding friends and discovering myself, but eventually joined a dating service in order to meet new people and create new friendships and relationships. I grew to become comfortable in my own space, without anyone else there. I wished it weren't that way, but I had to adapt. The place I was living in was a boarding house with tenants living in separate rooms. Soon after I moved in, one of the tenants left and Mauro moved into the vacated room. He was a good looking guy who loved the night life. He was always clubbing and going out with friends. I thought that he was going to be the one who would complete my life. I expected him to fill the missing gaps in my life and hoped that we could build a future together. I was deluding myself. We always went club hopping and just kept hanging out with the wild crowds and never made time to talk or get to know each other. This is not what I had in mind for a relationship and I felt like I was doing something wrong. He said nothing, did nothing toward growth and didn't stimulate me mentally at all. So we soon parted.

I've come to accept that my thoughts and actions are controlled by me, and not this illness within me. I am now thirty-eight years old and I feel I've lived a full life. I might not have enjoyed every moment of it, but I certainly wouldn't be who I am today if it wasn't for the trials I've had to wade through to get to this point in my life. I think, more often than not, about my young adult years and I think of everything that occurred during those times, and whether I would have changed anything if I could. Time flew so fast that I barely noticed its passing. I often stand in wonder of what my friends have done. It disappoints me some days, to look at all they've accomplished and I haven't even reached where I want to be yet. I had so many dreams and yet I cannot recall the last time I tried to realise one of them. I find comfort in the saying: 'It's not about getting there, but rather about the journey getting there.'

I look in the mirror in the morning and look at my grey hairs and think that at least I have proof of a full life. I am full of hope and hold a heart full of optimism for the future and what it may bring me. Loneliness still frequents me though. It watches over me as I go through each day. For what reason do I have to go through this? Will I ever be with the one that I love? I am constantly told that I need to be more available and that I need to remain positive. How do I clear my mind of the thought of being alone for the rest of my life? How do I deal with the obvious impending loneliness looming over me?

I am by no means saying that all gay relationships are lonely. I am saying that it is a lonely road to discovery and acceptance. Even though I have accepted myself, I cannot always let go of my problems. But every day I embrace opportunities and approach them openly and freely.

4

Somalian in need

The sun beats down on my far-away desolate country, as I sit in a rainy Cape Town. *Africa, my Africa! This is the place of my birth! This is my home!* I yearn to be in the northern part of the continent, the place of my birth. Somalia wants to hear none of this. It is filled with discrimination and prejudice against people like me. My state of being is not something that is acceptable to people of my country, especially to people of Muslim descent. Consequently, I have made South Africa my home. I am happy here, but still very uneasy. I have not yet totally adjusted, nor have I become comfortable and settled.

I sit watching the television and I see children swimming in the ocean like I did. They are running around in tattered and torn clothing that reminds me of my childhood of poverty. I appreciate the freedom that the ignorance of childhood allowed.

I really miss being with my family. My head spins in search of the thoughts of my achievements and accomplishments for my short existence on this planet. I cannot come up with anything. I try to think of what being this way has brought me, and all I can think of is pain, misery and heartache. But I am being unfair… there have been moments of happiness. Perhaps I should just tell my story and save myself from having to explain each detail, but then where should I start?

I know… A point of mystery and confusion. How does an eight-year-old boy understand why he is looking at other boys? Why is he not looking at girls like his friends are doing? At this

21

early stage in my life, my entire world started spinning around in circles. I was always at the beach with my friends or family and enjoying myself. My attention would always focus on the boys in their swimming trunks with their perfect bodies. Mine was not that perfectly structured. It all seemed so wrong. I was uncomfortable with this body that was given to me. I especially liked the tourists; the people with the white skins. I found them beautiful in a way that was like a child admiring a doll. It was all inherent of the indoctrination of believing that white people were superior to me. They also had the money and riches that I could not afford. Such was the power that they exuded. My family stopped going to the beach and so I would make my way there on my own, without really worrying about any dangers that might be lurking around dark corners. I enjoyed my days at the beach.

I always thought that my mind was playing tricks on me because I've never seen boys with boys before, so I thought there must be something wrong with me. At the age of thirteen I started asking questions. *Who am I? Why am I so different?* There were no answers. It could not be answered and I could not ask anyone about it because I was too afraid. I wondered if I was merely going through a phase. *Maybe I shouldn't think about it and it will go away.* The questions started branching out but the key question was always: *Why do I feel so awkward in this body of mine and why does my mind not seek companionship in a girl rather than a boy?* As the years flew by, I still could find no answers. I just couldn't figure it out. I could not sort out the monsters in my head.

My friends were only girls. One day, as we were playing in the streets, we saw a new family moving into the neighbourhood. We stopped our playing to watch them as they moved their things into their new home. Many of the local boys were running around, playing soccer and shouting at each other for kicking the ball in the wrong direction. They were normally our focus of discussion as we would usually laugh at them for being so stupid. Today they were forgotten as we transfixed our gazes at these new neighbours – a new family of five with three boys. This excited me because at this time I was a teenager and I was aware of the possibility of a new hope. There was the potential existence of a new friendship between myself and boys of my own age. The local boys rejected me during this era of my life as I did not play soccer with them. The potential realm of new possibilities subconsciously excited and stimulated my mind. Little did I know what the future held! They moved in right next door to my home. Hence, I thought we would naturally become friends. The group of friends soon became silent as they stood staring in awe at the new arrivals.

I tried making friends with the brothers, but they refused to talk to me. Even the adults just greeted me and walked away. At first the family looked down on ours because they came from a better part of the country. After much greeting and persistent efforts of getting to know them, the eldest son opened up to me and we started talking. This first encounter made him more at ease and he started to treat me with dignity and respect. His name was Karriem. He was built like an athlete with strong, large muscles. Soon we became better acquainted and he would greet me and we would have long conversations. The rest of his family would turn sour and sulk when they saw us together. They used to make fun of me and treated me like dirt. I couldn't understand what I had done to be treated like this. It just didn't make sense.

As time went on, Karriem's brothers also started to make fun of me at school with the rest of the children. They became even worse than the other children and instigated bullying strategies against me. I detested their unruly acts and deeds. I disliked them for this. Karriem provided comfort and relief. He would say that I should just ignore them and concentrate on my own life. His common saying was: 'They are stupid children and they will get nowhere in life, but you will travel and see the world one day!' Today, I realize that he was right. The bullying of the school children is what provided the opportunity for us to become friends. We spent more and more time together. Most of our free time was spent in each other's company. I was only too happy to spend my time like this. I also started developing strong feelings for him. I was scared to share this with him because I could not risk losing this first and only friendship that I had. I did not want to discover that he did not feel the same way as I did. I did not want to jeopardise our relationship. Our conversations meant everything to me.

Our lives were moving along swiftly, but it was interrupted by a civil war. This forced Karriem's family to leave the country. They left immediately when it started. It was sudden and without announcement. There was no time for goodbyes. All I had was a quick word with Karriem. I watched him flee with his family down the street. The next minute he was gone. I wished that things didn't have to be like this. I hated my life then. I couldn't deal with the issues that I was being confronted with. I felt saddened to see him leave. I hated this war. It swallowed my only bit of happiness. I lost my only friend in a moment of madness. *Would we ever be together again?*

Life in Somalia changed. Everything became very tense. There was a sense of busyness throughout the country. Everyone needed to be somewhere. The country wasn't doing so well. On any normal day, there would be this hustle and bustle. I loved it. Nobody seemed to notice me. I could get along with my own mundane existence. I guessed where everyone was going. What they were doing? No answer came to me. I would sit on the wall at the beach thinking about Karriem and what I felt for him. I tried to work through it, but could not. I missed him.

As the sun rose on my seventeenth birthday, my father told me that I needed to settle down and marry my cousin. I argued with him about this for days on end without any resolve. Eventually he just said: 'Well, you need to get married, so if you don't want your cousin, then you need to choose a decent girl from the community.'

24

I started getting worried, because my father was becoming insistent. I couldn't lie to him, but I also couldn't tell him the truth. How was I going to refuse my father?

As per custom and tradition, my father pressed on with arrangements and started his plans for the wedding. He had given his ultimatum. He wanted me to get married, and that was it! He expected what he said to be obeyed. In the community, the word of the elders demands conformity. He started making arrangements. This made me even more scared because I couldn't lie to myself or the girl that my father wanted me to marry. I had no options left. I stole money from my father, packed a few things and headed off to my grandmother. I hoped that she would be able to protect me from my father. Or rather the ideals that he wanted me to ascribe to. I hoped that she might be able to give me the answers that no one else was able to, or wanted to, give me.

She welcomed me with open arms. She thought that my father knew about this visit. She loved me very much and relished the time that she got to spend with me. We spoke of many things and she gave me advice that I desperately needed. I didn't tell her about the real reason that I had come, until she eventually asked me about it. She also wanted to know my future personal and career plans. I sighed heavily and finally told her why I left. I explained that I came to her because I wasn't ready to get married. I told her that my father was forcing me to get married to someone that I do not love. She said that I shouldn't run away from my problems, but to rather face them head on. I could not do this. My issues were far too sensitive and intricate for her to understand. It would also create another war if my father found out about my sexual identity. I didn't want to think about it. I asked my grandmother for some money and left for Yemen by boat.

I had family in Yemen. At first they were very happy to have me there. For a while, I stayed there with few problems. One day, my cousin got into some personal conflict with some people and they followed him home. This disrupted the entire household. The family was in disarray. The problem got so bad that they felt it best for me to leave as they had too many problems of their own. They could not be burdened with me being a part of their household. I left them and then travelled to Saudi Arabia.

The people there are very homophobic and I was afraid of what could happen to me if they discovered my sexual orientation. I could be killed. It was as if my every move was watched. I became very tired of living in fear. So, I decided to return home to Somalia.

As I made my way back home, I started worrying anew about the marriage events and wondered if my father would still want me to get married. When I got home, it was raining but for me it was a bright and sunny day because my father had moved to the United Kingdom. My mother was happy to see me home again and she rejoiced at the fact that I was back home safely. Life seemed good for a time, but it was not to last forever. My life quickly returned to the tedious routine lifestyle of my community. Generally, my day would start by helping my mother with what she needed, and then I would go to the beach and enjoy the view. One day while I was enjoying the view, some children who were at school with me poked fun at me. When I did not retaliate to their mocking and teasing, they beat me up. As I screamed for them to stop, they merely laughed and became more and more vicious. They left me lying on the ground, in the dirt, thinking that I was dead. When I got home, my mother went hysterical. She shouted at my siblings to help as she nursed my wounds. I was bed-ridden for several days. When I recovered, she suggested that I go to my family in Kenya. After thinking about my narrow escape from death and a second attack from the same group of people, I decided I needed to leave Somalia again.

Kenya provided little relief. It was almost the same as back home. I was merely grateful to be alive. After spending a few days there, I had a strange experience. Through the corner of my eye, I thought I saw someone that I recognised. On impulse I turned to look, but saw nothing. I just shrugged it off as seeing a ghost.

As the days rolled by, I hoped to find a way to escape the boredom that enveloped my new life. There were no employment opportunities in Kenya. I struggled to find a job so I just went about town trying to experience new things. I went to the coast one Saturday just to get my mind off all my problems. I sat with my feet in the water as I watched the tourists and sailors in their uniforms. I sat there for about half an hour and then noticed a familiar figure. It was the same guy I thought I had seen before. I stood up and walked his way. He started to walk in another direction and I followed. He turned a corner and I shouted out to him to come back. As I turned the corner, I was knocked of my feet as he came from the other side.

'I'm so sorry,' he said quickly, helping me up.

I looked up and saw the very same person that I thought it was. He stood looking at my awkward position as I got up from the ground. He stood staring at me in amazement. I stood staring back at him. It was Karriem. He was older and more mature, but his kind eyes hadn't changed. He smiled at me as he realised who I was. I went home with him and also told him that I was staying with my family. We shared some moments from the past. We laughed. It was the first time in a long time that I felt whole again. After several meetings, he suggested that I move in with him. I wasn't sure whether he was being serious. It seemed like heaven. When I confirmed with him, he said, 'I am so serious!'

He swiftly smiled at me and said, 'I'm alone in my place, so you can come stay with me. There are three more rooms at my place.'

I was so excited and wanted to hug him, but I had to remain composed. I was still unsure about what this meant. I was filled with so much confusion. *What if he didn't like me if we live in close proximity?* But I was filled with excitement and we immediately went to get my things. We got there about half an hour later. He showed me to my room and watched as I unpacked.

'You know,' he said, 'I've been in love with you ever since we met.'

I stopped and looked up at him, and saw he was being serious. I walked over to him, the clothing forgotten, and I kissed him. The connection that we shared there was phenomenal. He took my face in his hands and looked in my eyes. 'I hoped that you would –' I started to say, but he shushed me, and kissed me again.

From that time I was so happy and excited; I lost all sense of the stress and dangers that I had faced in Somalia. I was finally with the man I loved, and I intended it stay that way. He liked travelling so we travelled a lot around the country and he showed me things I had never dreamed of seeing. This was what I would like my life to be like, happy and with the person I love.

It all came to an abrupt halt when my aunt contacted me about a career opportunity in Cape Town. It was a difficult decision to make and it took an enormous amount of energy. I sat down and thought about this. Here I had the life I wanted, but I had no money. I needed to find my feet, especially with regard to employment, before I settled down. I wasn't ready to just stay at home and do nothing. I decided to go to my aunt in Cape Town and to work in her internet café. I was unhappy to leave Karriem. I felt that he was the person that I was meant to be with for the rest of my life, but not in Kenya.

Cape Town is a friendly city and I settled in very quickly. The people from my country were overwhelmed with my presence. They made every effort to make my stay a peaceful one. It went very well for a long time, and then came the fateful day when my aunt discovered some gay literature in my bedroom. I thought: *The audacity of her to go through my personal belongings.* However I could not say or do anything about it.

I was devastated and had nowhere to turn. My aunt told me that I was a sinner and that I should stay away from the family. She then spread the word to the entire Somalian community in Cape Town. It was impossible to find a place to live. She said that I was cursed and the family pronounced a death sentence on me. Her sons grabbed me and beat me up. I fled in panic. The men of the Somalian community were after me. They attacked me with sticks and stones. Eventually, I managed to get my things from her. This experience left me homeless again and alone. I wondered around aimlessly. I watched the beauty and splendour of Cape Town with people bustling around me, but it was a very lonely Cape Town. I fell into lapses of regret about leaving Karriem and Kenya. There was nothing left for me. I was at a loss and had to endure everything that came my way. Life became meaningless. I was desperate and alone!

Eventually, I landed up in Bellville. I stayed with some family friends that did not know about my sexual orientation. They were very nice people and I liked them very much, but this also came to an end when they found out about my sexuality. The worst part of it all was the manner in which they found out. One day when I attended *jumuah*, the Friday congregational prayer, at a local mosque, they threw me out because I was gay. They told me that I was filthy and I needed to be cleansed of my sins.

When I returned home the evening, the entire household had heard about my ordeal in the mosque. They fabricated a story that one of the sons was coming from abroad and they needed the room that I was staying in. So again, I found myself directionless and alone. I was once more destitute in Bellville, left to roam around the notorious Voortrekker Road, renown for prostitution and people living on the streets.

I was thrown out of my community, I had no refugee status and I was scared. I went to many organisations for assistance, but they would not help. Eventually I found one that helped me. They offered me a place to stay and I am still with them now. I am a volunteer and I enjoy where I am very much. What will happen after this I don't know, but I know that I'd like to remain happy. The only thing that can fulfil my happiness is being with Karriem. I pray that Allah will be with me and guide me on this road to where I'm supposed to be. I do not know what the future holds for me.

5

Living amongst the Queer

The sun rises on a brand new day, and the rays so easily filter through my curtains. I smile at the world, ready for another day, anxious for what it holds. I get up, do the toilet routine, and head down to the kitchen in my shorts and shirt. I live alone, so no chance of bumping into anyone. I make breakfast and watch television as I eat. I head to the bathroom and brush my teeth, take a shower and head back to my room to get dressed. I tighten my tie around my neck and study myself in the mirror. I look left to right, I check that I shaved properly, if my suit is clean and my shoes are polished. I go downstairs to the kitchen and dig out my pills from the back of the cupboard. I swallow them with some water, lock up and head for work. Once I get there, I'm as happy as can be, until I walk through that front door. The revolving door spins and I walk through readying myself for the onslaught. I walk in and greet everyone warmly, but I stay guarded. Many of them refuse to greet back, many refuse to even acknowledge my presence. They pull their noses up at me, look away, and feel that they are superior. I loathe them in that moment; in that moment that they act so childish and stupid; their ill-educated minds showing that they have no clue of what I am going through, never mind the rest of the nation. I get in the lift and all but a few decide they need to leave. I swear in my head and ask Allah for forgiveness and strength to not do it again. I reach my floor and head out into the landing where I take a left and continue down to my office. Everyone suddenly disappears into their offices, as if there's work to do at eight in the morning. I pretend not to notice and answer my cellphone as it vibrates in my pocket. It's my doctor wanting to know if I remembered my appointment for later that day, and I confirm. I hang up and continue to my office which is only two more doors down, but I'm stopped by a new girl.

'Mr Schultz wants to see you as soon as possible.'

I thank her and she passes me quickly, perhaps she's heard as well. I think about the manager wanting to see me, and I start wondering why. He is just as 'afraid' of me as these people are. I open my office; check my mail and leave to see the manager ten minutes later. I walk easily through the masses as they all make way for me by disappearing into their offices or the closest room or lavatory. I laugh inward; there is *some* enjoyment in their stupidity!

I knock as I approach the office and Mr Schultz says come in, so I do. His office is large, much bigger than my own, but you barely notice it because it is covered in paperwork and trophies and dead animal's heads are hanging around. His family portrait hangs on the wall behind him in an over-sized frame. I look at it as he indicates that I should sit down. I take the seat and wait for him to begin.

'It's my son's birthday today, so I need to be quick,' he says in his thick voice. His double chin wobbles a bit and a smudge of tomato sauce is still vacationing on it. I am disgusted by this man because you'd expect an employer to have respect for his employees, but not him. Not him.

I still wait without saying a word and watch him as he forces himself into his chair.

'The company has been thinking of adding a new branch to their collection and they wanted me to forward my choices to them of whom to put in this new branch.'

'I've selected you, Grant and Shanice as my three candidates. I've already spoken to them, and they are all aboard.'

I sat there thinking to myself: *Is this man trying to get rid of me?*

I could see him reading my face, and so he quickly decided to say something.

'The thing is, Imraan, that I feel that you and everyone would be happier if you weren't around each other anymore.' He stopped breathing heavily to regain what air he had just spent. 'Your AIDS problem has everyone so afraid of you that even our sales figures have gone down, and that's not good buddy. So you have two choices: either you choose to take the new job, or you leave the company completely. Start fresh on the other side.' He looked as if he was about to come around and pat me on the shoulder, but then he realised who he was talking to and stayed where he was. I sat there looking at him, fuming.

'I have to think about it,' I said.

'Why don't you take the week off then?' he said. 'In fact, I insist. Just give me a call on Friday to tell me what you've decided and we'll go from there.'

I was about to say something, but he stopped me.

'That's all.' He turned to look for something. 'I need to go, so if you'll excuse me...'

This was my cue to go, and I did, fairly quickly.

I didn't want to stay at this company any longer. I hated the way these people made me feel and I wondered if there would ever be a place where I'll be able to feel comfortable again. I picked up my things again and headed for home. I scolded about having to come there and then to go back home again.

Well at least I'm getting paid for doing nothing.

I decided to just head to the doctor and find out if he had any free time now, and he did. So he saw me and told me I should just keep doing what I've been doing, and I should be fine, but he couldn't guarantee anything. I left there totally tired of all the tests and grabbed a taxi home.

I got home fifteen minutes later and just sat on the couch channel surfing. I spent the rest of the day on that couch just snacking and watching television. I couldn't do anything else because the friends I thought were friends ran away even faster than my colleagues did and my family deserted me because I had slept with a lot of women. I was an imam and was rejected when they found out I was HIV-positive for the same reason, which was not even true. My wife had somehow gotten involved with drugs and she had slept with a few drug dealers to get what she wanted. I didn't know anything about this, so contracted the HI-virus from her. She obviously didn't admit to it, but I know she was the only person I've slept with. I started getting frustrated and got dressed. I left the house and just started walking. I went down a few blocks and then took a right turn and walked straight down. I started working through everything in my head. Is this a good job? Should I leave? Why should *I* have to leave because of their ignorance? This continued all the way down the street till I reached a park. I went in and sat on one of the swings. I pulled my coat tighter around me, not wanting to catch a cold. I could feel my blood rush to my face because of my anger, so I swung back and forth on the swing. I watched as the sky moved forward and backward above me and I felt relieved of the world; in that instant I had no worries. A heavy wind blew over and caught me unawares and I almost fell. I was shocked for a moment, but then couldn't help laughing at myself; *that was the funniest thing ever!*

I closed my coat again and steadied myself on the swing. The clouds overhead looked as though they were close to bursting and at that moment I felt the first drop. I smiled as it started drizzling, then raining. I stood there, absorbing as much as I could until the first sneeze came. My doctor would not be happy with me, because my immune system was already so low and now I still had to contend with the flu as well. I laughed and ran back the way I came and quickly found a café to duck into. It wasn't a cafe, however, but a bar. It was pouring outside now. I sat down at the bar and asked what they had that was warm.

'Coke!' was the only reply I got, which was followed by laughter. I ordered one and sat at the bar. I looked around a bit and saw that there were only three groups of people there, so it was very empty for this time of day. I checked my watch: 17:26.

I ordered another coke half an hour later, and when the rain still didn't let up, I decided I needed to make my way back. I got up and pulled on my coat again. I paid the bartender and on my way out I heard a whimpering, which sounded really sad. I stopped and pretended to be looking at the notice board but was actually listening in on this conversation.

'They kicked me out without blinking.' The guy actually sounded as if he were crying. I stopped to listen more.

'I went into my room, I had to grab everything and just everything –' he sniffed. He took a sip of something, and then continued. 'My mom was crying her lungs out and my dad was screaming *his* lungs out and my brothers were just happy to see me go. At first, I was shocked by this reaction, but then I realised I'd been expecting this to happen all along. I don't know why I was so shocked by it.' Someone patted him on the back, and they seemed to be fiddling with his jersey, because I could hear the rustle of the material. I moved my finger from article to article on the board, making as if I were interested. I made as if my cell was ringing and answered, talking to an imaginary friend on the other side. I walked back to one of the smaller tables and ordered another coke, and said, 'Oh no. What happened?'

'Really?' I asked the phone. 'So you're not coming? That's too bad.'

After another long pause, I said goodbye and hung up.

I sat just behind that group and I could hear every word. I would've liked to tell that guy that I knew exactly what he felt like, but I didn't know what his dilemma was, and even then, you don't just talk to strange people in bars.

My coke came and I started playing with my phone. Some of the guys left from the table to go to the toilets and only three of them stayed and they started gossiping. I watched the other set move away and I noticed one of them had a slight flair in their walk, and I realised what they were. I was so shocked at myself that I nearly fell off my chair.

They are GAY!

I almost wanted to slap myself in the face, but then I stopped. I thought about all the things I had to go through with my HIV which I didn't choose, and what they have to go through with their sexuality, which is part of who they are. I was so all over the place today that I didn't even realise that one of them had noticed me going loopy?

'Are you okay?' he asked me, and I saw it was the guy who was moping earlier. I assured him I was.

'Are you sure?' he insisted, and I just nodded.

'Wait,' I said as he walked away.

'I kind of know what you're going through and I've never realised that you guys had to deal with so much,' I said quickly. 'I'm sorry I ever felt that I should distance myself from you, and I now see that there is no real difference between a straight guy and a gay guy. Allah made us all, and Allah will take us all away.'

I felt good after getting that off my chest and I was ready to leave, but this guy had other plans for me.

'You want to sit with us?' he asked me.

I looked at the rest of the group and they were as inviting as he was. I started getting worried, and said I was about to leave.

'Surely you can stay a few more minutes and talk to us?' he asked me.

I tried to think of a way out of it, but couldn't so I decided to sit down and have one last coke with them. They wanted to know my life story, and as strange as it may seem, I shared it with them. There was something about the way they were that made me feel that I could trust them, and as soon as I did I felt amazing because they didn't shun me, they didn't run away or hide, they didn't even flinch. They started talking about people they knew who had full blown AIDS who were still out partying and had had it for thirty years. I enjoyed this meeting and the one coke quickly became many because I started falling into their conversation and they didn't even bring up men. They discussed politics, movies, what happened at the club, whatever; the range of topics were varied. I couldn't remember the last time I had shared with anyone, not to mention an entire group of people. Before we left, they invited me to this function they were having at a friend's place, and I happily agreed. We left, the one offered me a ride home and there were three of us in the car and I sat in front with him. They dropped me in front of my house and I went to bed happy. I didn't even mull over anything, I didn't fret about anything – I just showered, changed and went to bed, unconcerned about my past.

All I wanted at that moment was to feel that good and I wanted to bask in the feeling. I wanted to soak up the happiness and drink away the last however many years that I have left, to live my life in misery because of my family, my friends and my job.

I decided the next day that I'd buy a paper and I was going to sit at the computer with a list of ideas for a new job. I can't keep going through a working environment unhappy.

I loved myself again and I was so happy Allah had finally made me realise that all I needed to do was love myself and no one else could make me feel bad.

The next morning I did exactly that. I went to the shop bought three newspapers and I went on the net and surfed for work. I had three instant replies and I set up interviews for Thursday and Friday. I was totally happy with the result. I called into my old job and I told them they can let me go if they want to, but I'm expecting quite a big package for leaving. After all they wanted me to leave. On Friday I was offered one of the jobs and I waited until the following week to decide which of the two call-backs I wanted and I started three weeks later. As for my friends in the gay community, we became even better acquainted and I got to know so much more about them and their lifestyles. I also met many vibrant, loving people who accepted people for who they were. They had no hang-ups about their friends, they accepted them for who they are, regardless of what kind of lives they have lived.

Allah had finally showed me that I AM LOVED!

6

A secret well kept

Manenberg is sometimes regarded as a hotspot for crime. Tonight the heat was definitely not radiating from Manenberg. The street was amok with the chaos and confusion as people stood gathered around the ambulance. The air of mystery was all around. The community was bewildered by this healthy woman who laid spread out on a stretcher. She just got married the day before. The lingering question on everyone's lips and in everyone's minds was 'What happened?' Someone in the crowd lewdly exclaimed in a guttural Afrikaans something that roughly translates into, 'Possibly there was too much consummation of the marriage! It must have been too much for her! She possibly overdid herself!' This was the brutal humour and mentality that depicts the community.

Miema was an ordinary Muslim lady like any other. She was pious, attended *madressa* in the afternoons, loved to wear her *hijab,* fasted in the month of Ramadan and was very soft natured. She was the kind of girl that any Muslim parent, pious or not, would have been proud of. She was no angel and definitely had her shortcomings, but always strived to be the kind of person that would please Allah. She even finally fulfilled the family wish by getting married to a well-reputed man in the community. He was steadfast in his beliefs and was a true ambassador of Islam. *What could possibly have happened to her? Why is she being rushed to hospital?*

She had a secret, a secret that was not even known to her closest friends and family members. After all it was a secret, so how could they have known. It was all hush-hush. No one suspected a thing. She felt that she was safe. She knew that she would be rejected by her family if they knew. The community would ostracise her if the truth came out. Although she felt safe, she still had this inner fear that someday, someone would find out about *'it'*. She vowed to herself that she would overcome it and that she would never have to disclose her inner being, the essence of what she was. She even punished herself for it by eating extremely salty custard that she made for herself whenever she felt that she transgressed. She did this even when she felt close to transgression. These were the strong values that were instilled in her. *So what was this secret that she was keeping from everyone? Was it really all that bad?*

She used to stand and make long *raka'ats* of *tahajud* during the latter part of the night and on top of that she fasted every Monday and Thursday. She went as far as fasting on the thirteenth, fourteenth and fifteenth of each lunar month to ask Allah to free her from this *'sin'* that she was born with. She tried many things to fight it but to no avail. There were times that she lost hope, but because of her staunch religious beliefs, suicide was never an option. This thought had crossed her mind several times. After all she was just a normal human being with feelings, fears and emotions like everyone else. If suicide was not an option how on earth would she then be able to cope with this enormous 'burden' that she was keeping to herself, this thing that gave her sleepless nights and made her lose her appetite? What was she supposed to do to take herself out of the heaviness that she so often felt?

A friend of a friend of Miema's fell in love with her and wanted her to be his girlfriend. She was very reluctant, but thought that it might be a manner of getting the community off her back. So even though it was against Miema's personal beliefs and values to be deceitful, she decided to go for this guy. After all she did share a plutonic love for him and they became good friends. Besides, she saw this as another opportunity to fix this 'thing' that she was sitting with. As time progressed, he became more like a brother to her and their relationship grew even stronger. Albeit that she still did not love him as one loves a life partner. Part of her culture from her Indian background still practiced arranged marriages; so, she was very amenable to a marriage with the possibility of nurturing her feelings for her partner after they got married. She believed that it was possible to develop an intimate affection for each other over time. Even though their relationship developed to a deeper level she did not completely open up to him. She could not tell him what her secret was. The belief was firm in her heart that she would overcome 'it'. Two and a half years later, he proposed marriage to her and she accepted. She really believed that this was the answer to her prayers. Finally this 'thing' would disappear and she would be able to forget about it for good and move on with her life.

A few months later, the marriage took place. Everyone was excited, especially Miema's husband. He had waited for this for a long time. They were together for almost three years and weren't sexually involved with each other before due to their Islamic beliefs. He could not wait to get home that night so that they might get to know each other. She on the other hand was very nervous and did not want to be with him in that way. He respected her wishes and did not pressure her.

That night she waited till he fell asleep, got up, took *wudu* and started praying to Allah. She was very distressed because she was still sitting with this 'thing' that she silently started to accept, but did not want to give in to it due to her religious beliefs. She cried profusely and begged for answers. That night, according to her, Allah was not listening to her anymore. She felt extremely hopeless and for the first time seriously considered suicide. She went into a panic attack and shouted for her husband to help. She became heated up from inside because of fear for Allah's punishment and thought that she was being punished for thinking of killing herself. As her husband bent over to help, she lost consciousness and laid sprawled out on her *musallah,* quiet as a mouse. He managed to revive her and she said that her condition was brought on by the stress of planning the wedding. He left it at that and they went to bed. She could not sleep and tossed around for most of the night. She could not bring herself to share her secret with anyone and it was now becoming unbearable.

The next night her husband wanted to sleep with her and she decided to just go with the flow because this might help her. Maybe, just maybe this time around, the help of Allah would come. As he was about to enter her, she screamed and rolled to the other side of the bed. Her husband was confused and came closer to her to comfort her and find out what is wrong. She pushed him away from her and got up out of the bed. She became manic. 'I'm a lesbian, I can't do this anymore,' she shouted. 'I'm very sorry but I just can't do this anymore.' She started speaking as if in tongues. She cried hysterically and went into another panic attack, heavier than the one she had on the previous night.

He was perplexed, his facial expressions revealing a series of emotions. It changed from fear, to worry, to deep confusion. This all happened in a matter of seconds. If it wasn't a serious matter, I am sure that any onlooker would have burst out laughing. 'You are imagining things,' he said as he rushed out of the bungalow to go to the main house for help. As he dashed out, she collapsed into a stupor. Not long after that the ambulance arrived and it became known to them that she had a nervous breakdown.

So there she lay in full view of the entire neighbourhood. She lay in the back of an ambulance en route to the nearest government hospital. This is the easy hurdle to cross, the difficult one would be when she returns after the visit to the hospital.

She stayed there for almost three weeks. After she came out of the hospital, she did not want to go back home. She saw it as her husband's place; it did not belong to her. She took her belongings and moved back to her mother's place. The hospital placed her under therapy and she had to attend weekly counselling sessions. The counselling gave her an enormous amount of strength and courage. She started feeling stronger and more comfortable within herself as time went on. A few months later she decided to make things right with her husband. She wanted to provide him with clarity around the situation and to update him about what was happening. She did love him, but merely as a friend and thus she wanted to assist him to go through the predicament that she felt she placed on him. They had a long conversation and he kept on saying that he would be able to help her through her issues. She was steadfast in her decision. She knew that staying married to him was definitely not an option. He took it very hard but respected her wishes and politely asked her to leave.

Her parents were extremely hurt and could not accept her 'state', as they called it. They put her out of the house. They were deeply disappointed in her and it was as if they had forgotten all about her goodness. Being a lesbian was the only side of her that they saw. They could not relate her to the staunch practicing Muslim girl that performed her daily prayers each day. They could no longer see the girl who had Allah in her heart. She found herself wondering why they were so harsh. She had an uncle that drank, a brother that never performed prayers. Yet no one in the family directly condemned their behaviour as strongly as they did with her sexual orientation. Her cousins were thieves and gangsters, but no one commented as much about that. Why are the things that they do out of choice not as bad as her innate being? This is something she had no control over, something she didn't choose. These were all questions that went through Miema's head as she packed her stuff to move to her friend's place in Woodstock. Her 'pious' mother spat and swore at her as she left: 'Do not bother to come back until you have made *taubah* and changed your evil ways.'

As Miema took her last walk out of her parent's house, with her suitcase in her hand, she greeted her family: 'I would rather stay at a friend's place and be myself, than stay in this home of hypocrisy. I still love you all very much and I will make *duah* for you to see Allah's wisdom! I love you. As *salaam hu alaikum*! May peace be with you!'

Since that day she never looked back once. She never rekindled her relationships with her family, but built new ones. She continued to go for counselling and was later also referred for spiritual counselling and guidance. Miema became strong once more and strived towards strengthening her relationship with Allah. Her husband finally realised that she would never modify her behaviour and come back to him, so he agreed to a divorce.

Much later in life, Miema met and fell in love with a Muslim lady. They developed and still share a beautiful relationship. This gave her more courage to go on with life.

Miema firmly believes and feels that the orthodox way of thinking played a big role in her mental ordeal. For a long time she believed that if she accepted herself for being a lesbian, then Allah would punish her. This orthodox voice eventually proved to be very negative to her well-being. Only when she started to believe that the best way to get to know Allah is to get to know and understand herself first, could she begin to have a sincere and authentic relationship with Allah. Allah created each of us with a purpose in mind and when we pretend to be what we are not, then we are destroying Allah's plan for our lives.

She is now secure in herself and can be seen every Friday at a progressive mosque for *jumuah*, the congregational prayer.

7

Brothers

While I was sitting in the park with my mom and dad, I saw a strange sight. A group of peculiar looking men walked past us. Some were wearing women's clothing and they all seemed to walk in a funny way. As they continued they stopped and observed their surroundings. They were very observant but somehow appeared pensive and distracted. There were some that just seemed to float with the crowd without doing anything.

I asked my parents who they were because they looked so weird. They both started speaking simultaneously and nervously. My overprotective mother said something about them being performers in a show at the local theatre. I always thought it would be so much fun to become an actor. Their faces however seemed to become irritated at the harsh, yet embarrassed stares of my parents. The change of disposition was sudden and I was not fully aware of their discomfort and the reason for their mood swings. These people were exquisite. It was the first time I had ever seen people that looked so fashionable. I liked their style and their flair. They were better looking than any girls that came to mind. 'It is not always the girls that are best dressed,' I thought. Fifteen minutes later, we were out of the park and back onto the noisy streets of the suburbs.

I felt so angry at my parents because we were supposed to spend the entire day at the park. They, however, feared the unknown. There were never any family discussions or insinuations, but everyone always suspected that I was gay. I, on the other hand, never had any encounters with the gay world and never had any understanding of it. In fact my sexuality was never an issue. I laugh to myself now about how naïve I was. My thoughts were always based on my little cocoon-like world.

From that moment on my life was rather mundane until the death of my father. He was in a car accident. I don't know the full details because my mother could never fully confront the situation. She never shared the details of what happened. She merely said that there was an accident. I had to accept it for what it was. The funeral service was tragic. Everyone in the church stood heartbroken. I was the eldest of three brothers and we were all still very young. We felt for our mother and became protective towards her. We understood her state of being and thus for a long time we just stayed out of her hair; giving her some time to deal with and adjust to my father's death.

About a year later she met a man and dated him for a while. He was a burly man and well built. He was kind, funny and sweet too. It was evident that he made her happy. He didn't mind us and sometimes took us out on our own, or played games with us. I thought this was very unusual. My experience was that men don't usually do these things. They run away and shirk their responsibility of engaging with children, especially if they are not their own. It was my understanding that they do not take care of things that are not their own. We, as children, are merely possessions of the male adult world. This information, I gathered from the salons, dentists, vets, everywhere! My world said that women always have issues about men and their relationships with children. This man shattered our perceptions of men. He was different. He really cared. Our entire circle of friends said the same thing about him. He seemed different!

Although everyone agreed that he was an amazing man, as siblings we spent a lot of our time discussing if he's okay for *our* mother. This was a daily ritual amongst us. We were concerned for our mother's well-being because it naturally affected ours as well. She was also a gem of a person, had a heart of gold and deserved the best in life. She loved this odd man and they were magic together, so he passed our tests. We accepted that they would get married and they did. The warmth of this man made my mother decide to follow his way of life. He was pure and he had an extremely positive energy that was filled with peace. She adopted Islam as our family belief system. This shift was not done for him, but rather because of him. We stopped going to church, but my mother did not want to force her new religion onto us. We didn't see anything wrong with all the new changes in our lives as we were only about eight years old and younger at the time. Life was beautiful and this new family way of life seemed like a dream come true. There was always a beautiful smell of incense and an oriental feel to our new home. He became our father; he was an exemplary role model and a great inspiration for our household.

A year after the marriage, I developed a keen interest for this mystical religion. When he asked if I wanted to accept it as my way of life, I felt a sense of pride and belonging. I was now more like him and I adored his wonderful ways. Obviously we did not understand much about Islam and did not adopt all the rigid traditions and customs. We merely took it in our stride. I enjoyed my new journey into Islam and attended a Muslim school to learn more. I enjoyed it at first. Later I found that I was not truly connecting. There were times that I just didn't feel spiritually connected. Another source had filled my being. I had developed a nervous energy; an element of uncertainty and confusion entered my soul. I could not place my finger on this state of confusion. This condition took a more mystifying turn when I reached puberty. I did not comply with the custom of being attracted to girls. All my friends had begun speaking about the wondrous world of girls. My family was teasing me about my class mate being 'my girlfriend'. I could not identify with all the new absurdity that surrounded my space. It was necessary to pretend to understand the stories, but it was impossible to apply it to my being. It did not fit! I was befuddled! But somewhere in my subconscious there was a sense of knowing.

Life went on as if there was nothing different about me. Teenage life focussed on existing and getting through each day; attending classes, visiting friends, listening to music, socialising. I did what I had to do, and I followed my dad's example and guidance. Other children excelled and I just got by with everyday life. There was merely emptiness and longing. At the time, I did not know what was behind this apprehension towards life as an adolescent. If only my *psyche* could speak out and tell me about the unknown, the hidden. My life was like an abyss.

Graduation from high school came and went. All I recall is sitting in the school hall and waiting for my certificate. I sat next to my two best friends, Shanaaz and Faried, as they called out the names for best performances throughout the year. They both laughed at the nerdy children who were going up to accept their awards and I just smiled at them wondering what the next step of life would hold. After the ceremony, we left together to prepare for the dream of most school-leavers, The Matric Ball, the equivalent of the American prom. This was uneventful. We then dropped my date, my young niece, who was keen to attend because she had an eye on Faried. He had a girlfriend but also enjoyed the extra attention that she showed. We then made our way to an after party, which was the usual type of teenage party. I was not familiar with this lifestyle but attended because it was customary to do so. After all, I had just graduated.

As we socialised, I met a lot of people that I had merely seen in passing. And then life took a twist.

During the evening, the cooldrinks pressed on my bladder, knocking for an outlet. I was a strange lad that only practiced my toilet routine in family facilities. I was nervous about using public or other places, but this was an emergency. There was no need to excuse myself from the company as everyone was free spirited. So this was my maiden voyage into a public toilet. I was relieved to see that it was empty, so I passed the urinal to enter a cubicle. My modest nature stemmed from the Islamic teaching of seeing the lower body as a private region that should not be exposed in public. I went in and just before I could close the door, another boy pushed his way in and closed the door behind him. I stood aghast and thought maybe he was running away from someone, but he turned around and looked at me intently. He leaned against the door and locked it and came toward me. I took a step back, not knowing what to expect. I moved back with every step he took toward me.

I knew him from school, but in shock I asked, 'Who are you? What do you want?'

He smiled gently and my stomach took a turn, 'I'm Imraan, and I want you,' he said.

I couldn't understand this, he looked so normal. I remember him as a good Muslim. I took another step backwards and landed my bottom on the pot. Instinctively I jumped from there as if it had bitten me. I forgot my need, grabbed him and kissed him intensely. Yes, there in the cubicle. I could not understand it. My head spun in circles. I pushed him away and asked him to leave. I think I may have smacked him. I needed to be alone. He left. I emptied my bladder. I washed my face, rubbing my lips with cold water. I rubbed hard as if it was dirty. I looked up into the mirror. I saw someone else. It wasn't me. It was someone else in the mirror. In that instant it was confirmed! I was attracted to boys and not to girls. I still did not understand it. I was trying to find a way to explain it to myself because I couldn't ask anyone without revealing my secret. I made an attempt at rationalising it.

It was clear, my years of oblivion stemmed from denial. I remember the thoughts that I hid when I found myself drooling over the boys at school and wishing that I could kiss them. I stood there, appreciating what God created. I loved myself. I wanted to run out and tell the world of my discovery. I felt free. I was alive. Life came gushing through my veins.

Although the kiss was quick and my lips were scrubbed, I could still feel the kiss of Imraan. My heart raced and my body quivered at the thought. How did he realise? What gave him the indication that I would respond? How did he know? Could it be that everyone knew about my sexuality, except me. No, subconsciously I knew about it, but kept it to myself. I couldn't speak about it because I thought that if my family found out, it would probably be the end of my relationship with them. I also had never known about anyone else who was like me.

There was a sudden silence as Imraan came back into the bathroom. He started to apologise.

'Stop there,' I said, a little uncertain. 'I don't know what you're thinking but it can't be right.'

'I know I'm right, Shamsoedien.' My name being said in such a way was a new thing for me. I held onto the hope that someone would walk in and I wouldn't have to confront this issue. He was in front of me before I knew it and I had no control over the situation. It was just happening. He pressed himself against me and I tried to move, but as soon as I did, he pushed me against the wall and his leg brushed against mine. He then looked into my eyes, and I knew that there was terror in them. My heart was beating profusely and I couldn't restrain him as he pushed his lips against mine. He held me against the wall, and as soon as his lips touched mine I melted. There was no fighting this as it was a part of me and the sooner I accepted it, the better. My mind was lost to the world as I savoured the emotions that filled me. This all just felt so right, how could it possibly be wrong?

At the end of that night, I had had my first sensual kiss. In that moment that I kissed Imraan, I accepted who I am, and I promised myself to not hide it ever again. When I got home that evening I still had adrenalin flowing through my veins. I felt powerful, invincible and indestructible. I went to my parents and asked them to just sit down because I needed to speak to them before I lost my nerve. I called my brothers as well, and they took seats around my parents. They were all a bit worried now as to what could warrant a family meeting at this time of night.

'I know that it's late, so I'll try to make this as short as possible,' I said. I walked around them and continued talking.

'I have been struggling with something for my entire life, and I need to just get it off my chest.' I took a moment to ready myself for what was coming, before I said what I wanted to say. 'I am gay,' I said.

Everyone who was sleeping a few moments ago was now wide awake. From the chilling silence there was a muffled, confused and guttural 'Huh!?'

This was all that came from the people in the room.

'I'm gay,' I said again. 'I've known for a while now but was always afraid to tell you. Tonight I realised that I cannot keep hiding it, if I want to live my life to the full.'

My dad looked at me for a while and then spoke. 'I've always known there was something different about you, but I never thought this.' I stood there looking at him as he started to lift himself. He stood there a moment and said, 'Well, I guess we'll just have to accept it as it's not really a choice. It's part of who you are.'

I was so glad for these words that I grabbed him and hugged him tightly. My mother, who was smiling now, hugged me tightly, and then followed her husband to the room. I also watched my brothers saunter to their rooms.

I thought that everyone would need a lot of time to deal with this new information. The following day, however, my brothers mocked me and asked why it took me so long to realise my sexuality. We laughed for a while about it and I was finally happy. I was comfortable with whom and what I am and my feelings didn't feel wrong anymore.

Time flew by. I had developed a very strong relationship with Imraan. We were very happy together and everyone accepted our bond, but never spoke about it.

Zubayr, my youngest brother and the only child born from this wedlock, had now completed school, was working and was ready to engage fully with the world of adulthood. He had a strong faith and bond with Allah. My dad was very traditional with him, more so than with the rest of us who came from a

Christian background. I guess dad silently hoped that Zubayr would uphold Muslim Indian traditions.

One day dad announced to the family that he had met a girl that he wants to arrange for Zubayr to get married to her. He explained that this union would create a strong bond between the two families. Zubayr appeared nervous and Dad called him to the kitchen to chat. A moment later, it was as if a thunderstorm hit our house. Dad was out of the house in a flash; into his car and he sped into the night. This was unlike him. He was disturbed. I made my way to my brother in the kitchen as my mother made her way to the bedroom. I sat down next to him in the kitchen. His head was placed on the cold marble covering of the counter as his sobs echoed in the room. I ran my fingers through his hair. For a while we remained silent as we took in each other's emotions. Eventually he sighed deeply as he looked up at me.

'Was it difficult for you?' he asked me, slowly turning his face towards me. I continued stroking his hair as we shared a knowing silence. Speaking with our eyes was common practice between us. We often knew what the other was saying. Words were not always needed. He started speaking as if to himself, and slowly too, 'Tell me again about your night of coming out. How did dad take it? I was sleeping when you revealed everything.'

'It was difficult, but then when I did it, it felt amazing,' I told him. 'I felt empowered and the family accepted me almost instantly,' I reminded him.

'Why?' I asked him. 'Did you tell Dad?'

'That I'm gay?' he said quickly, for fear of not being able to say it.

'Yes,' I said as I looked at him. I lifted him, hugged him and told him it was all okay.

'But why would he accept *you* so easily? Why is it so difficult to accept me?' He asked, tears welling up in his eyes.

'Give it time,' I said. 'Give him time.'

I was the only one in the family that knew that Zubayr was

gay, but I left it for him to share it with the family when he was ready. After a while, as we left the kitchen, we could hear my dad in the room with mom. She was consoling him. My brothers were sitting on the couch waiting to hear the news. We just sat there embracing each other until one of my other brothers exclaimed, 'Oh, my goodness. I should have known.'

He had a sick sense of humour and he burst out laughing as he commented: 'Shams, if you were not brothers and you were not involved, I would have sworn that the two of you were lovers.' He burst out laughing at his own joke. All the brothers laughed and that was all that was needed to ease the atmosphere. Soon we were sharing past stories and experiences.

It was not as easy after that. Father refused to speak to Zubayr and a wedge formed between them. Eventually they weren't communicating at all. My mother was at a loss and she didn't know what to do about the situation. My brother was staying out till late so that he didn't have to speak to my father. He focused more on his Islamic studies and pretended to go on as normal. The family didn't see him as often as they used to, which didn't make sense at all. I could see my mother's pain, my father's suffering and the confusion of Zubayr. I spoke to my parents and told them that their responses affected the entire family because everyone was emotionally connected to the two of them. Dad just sat there and looked through me as I spoke. It was as if I was invisible. I looked at him, and tried to think of what to say to encourage him. He looked so lost and he didn't seem to register what was around him. I could see that this was having a negative impact on him.

'I know I need to be there for him because otherwise he's just going to avoid us, but I don't know if I can do this,' he explained. 'I'm not sure how to handle the situation.' He could not explain the reason for his current state and I did not want to push him into a corner. So, we merely left it at that in the hope of continuing the conversation at a later stage.

The next day Zubayr shared with me, 'I don't want to be

chastised and judged by dad or anyone else. I have Allah with me and in my heart. So, I don't see why I need to entertain anybody else's opinion about my life and sexuality.'

I tried to find a way to get my dad to talk to Zubayr but nothing seemed to work. Eventually one of our brothers intervened. He forced Zubayr into the house and sat him down with my father in the dining-room. They sat looking at each other for a while and then finally spoke. They shared their issues and expressed their feelings and thoughts with one other. It was intense and we had to often prevent them from leaving the room. Both of them were soon shedding buckets of tears and they finally hugged one other.

I was happy that my family was finally okay again. I hoped that things would stay that way. There are so many things that we, as gay people, have to go through to be ourselves. Sometimes it seems so frivolous to get into fights about little things with our loved ones. I hold onto the hope that we will live comfortably until the end of our lives. Hopefully one day we will create a world that is free of judgement; a world where it is not considered wrong to be true to one's sexual identity.

8

A road less travelled

At the tender age of sixteen I was forced to ponder more closely on that burning adolescent issue – *my* sexuality! If the truth be told I had always felt older than what I was and experienced a peculiar feeling of displacement. Like the typical teenager whose sexual inquisitiveness and exploration starts in the early teens, I sought my education in books, friends and the media. Sixteen is a difficult year for many people; not quite an adult yet but old enough to know something is different.

Now, my relationship with my father was virtually non-existent as he had no contact with me for most of my life and having been raised (most of the time) by my over-zealous, God-conscious mother. I was moulded to be the perfect product of her fanatical dogma. I felt awfully dislocated, ill-at-ease and racked with guilt. I had an undeniable sense of inconsistency and insecurity throughout my developing years due to the frequency with which we moved from one location to another; just Mother and I.

So it was this exploratory year, when I could no longer ignore my attraction to males, that I sought help from my biology teacher. I don't know why I chose him, but I guess it must've been the association to our lessons about the human anatomy. His approach was sensitive and sympathetic but no less dogmatic. It would be a few years before I would truly come to terms with my preference for male sexual partners. He did, however, help me identify this burgeoning awareness, because up until then, I hadn't a clue I was gay! After having united my Hyde with my Jekyll, believe me when I say, all I wanted to do was shout it from the rooftops! It was something exciting to discover and accept who I am.

Unfortunately I am not gifted in hiding who I am. My mannerisms were a bit effeminate to say the least. It had been this way for all my life. I was stoned, literally every day, by the neighbourhood kids and pelted as often with cans, food, chalk, pieces of pavement. In fact, with whatever could be used as a throwing device. This was usually accompanied by a few memorable remarks – forever seared on a young man's memory. On a good day I'd walk away with more than my fair share of insults. As the abuse became more daring, the bruises became less obvious. The wounds were all on the inside. The agony of feeling vulnerable and unprotected was a constant companion. *I was afraid.*

I had started relating to my homosexuality and religion as an affliction that I would not be able to shake off. For God's sake, I was both a born-again Christian and homosexual! What would mother say?! I believed that I was surely going to hell. Since I could not marry these two aspects of myself, let alone exist within a duality of this nature, I chose to forego and disavow the God of my mother. I was alone.

Weighed down with depression and seeing no way out, I convinced myself that I was clearly a mistake, an anomaly. And within three days I had decided to rid the world of me and I planned my suicide. A bottle of water and twenty painkillers later, I found myself in a wheelchair. Somebody had found me, where I lay unconscious, and then rushed me off to hospital.

The doctors managed to save me from myself. My mother popped in to make sure I hadn't died, then hastily took off again... I love my mother more than she will ever know, but I don't think she knew how to deal with me and with what was happening. This hurt and I had an intense sense of hopelessness. Two weeks later I slit my wrist. That, clearly, also failed. Leaving the house to go to school in the morning was terrifying, because I knew exactly what my day would be like. Honestly, the persecution I faced from the world around me was endurable. The rejection I faced by my mother was not. Growing up, I wasn't told I was good enough just the way I was or encouraged to express my ideas, my feelings, my perspectives. I was told to be more like other boys. Mother continually reminded me that I was a disappointment and an embarrassment to my family. It was because of my shameful nature that I was also kicked out of my home. She unceremoniously packed my clothes in black bags and shoved me out. I faced the hard task of having to find a place to stay. I was confused. She was my mother. But my mother did not want me. I decided she did not love me.

I felt I had nowhere else to turn but to others for guidance. I was vulnerable and felt small, angry and lost. Kind friends took me in. I worked whenever I could find work and took counsel and solace from my friends. Unfortunately my sense of goodness had been damaged and I was slow to realise that some of these friends were taking advantage of me. Their world was unfamiliar to me. It was a world where drugs, money and sex were the gods. Soon I was dabbling in drugs and prostitution. Not long after that I was addicted to drugs and prostituting my body. I needed to belong. After nearly five years of relocating I went back to my family and stayed with my grandmother. She totally accepted me and cared for me and for a while all seemed well with me. But I had so many unresolved issues and they were slowly but surely straining to the surface. The fact that I was not yet 'out' with regards to my sexuality, having to explain why I didn't have a girlfriend, my AIDS scare, a failed long-term relationship to which I was very attached, and 1-2-3, I was back on anti-depressants.

My methods of old weren't working anymore. I was exhausted. I was only twenty-three years old and I was exhausted. The world had betrayed me, my lover had left me and my mother lived as if I had never existed.

To whom could I turn? To the God that I had abandoned so many years ago? No! I couldn't. I couldn't go back to the God of my mother, for look at what kind of mother she had become, and yet she was an ardent believer. Yet, I couldn't seem to carry myself anymore. It became clear to me that I needed a God.

It was at this time that I came upon an organisation that dealt with the issues that had been plaguing me. I approached the employees desperately looking for further education, enlightenment and support on this arduous and uncharted journey that was my life as a homosexual male. They never judged me. They understood entirely the need in me to know God without having to relinquish how I chose to love someone.

Did I mention that my father's Muslim by birth? Anyway, I started investigating the God of my father (so to speak) and what I found was more than I had bargained for. I had discovered a world, a way of life that held within its rituals and rhymes such beauty and peace. My preconceptions of a faith misunderstood were shattered. I was indescribably humbled by what I was learning and an unfamiliar sense of God was beginning to unfurl within me. I threw myself into it, socks and all. I found hope again at a time in my life when I believed I was dying. And I have not looked back since. Embracing Islam was the best change in my life.

Do you wonder how it is that I can accept being homosexual and Muslim? I believe that Allah will judge me as he sees fit on the Day of *Qiyamat*. And may Allah have mercy on my soul that I do not believe that who I am is wrong but has led me inexorably to this point in my life *subhannallah*. I have never felt more whole and I have never felt more peaceful.

All praise be to God.

9

Mistaken identity

'What's in a name?' This was the first question they asked me in the interview process, and I looked at the interviewer laughing. I felt a bit uncomfortable as I had never spoken to this person about my life before. But I am accustomed to talking about my life. It has been a long journey. Although there are times when I say and feel like I don't really have that much to share; people always tell me that I'm wrong. They say that my life is filled with a lot of important information that could possibly help others. I smile at the interviewer and explain to him that my name means 'handsome' and I giggle. I continue to tell him that my selected name is a Persian one, which means 'totally in order'. The reason I chose this name was because I felt as if everything in my life was right now; I felt complete and in order. We laughed a bit and then got started on my childhood. Maybe I should just share this; I think it will be less confusing and easier to understand.

I spent the first twenty-four years of my life in Bonteheuwel, schooling there until the beginning of my working days. I went to Bergsig Primary School and I enjoyed it there. I was already a bit effeminate when I started school so obviously, living in a township, derogatory names trailed me everywhere. I was called every name in the book, but because I was a strong- minded child, it was like water off a duck's back. I never let the teasing get to me unless someone was strongly abusive and it irritated me. Although my retaliation often escalated the problems, I never let other people's opinions affect me as they did not have to live my life.

I've always attended *madressa* and never missed any of my classes. My father became a caretaker at the mosque and he then became part of the establishment. I was always expected to be the replacement for him when he was not available to do things at the mosque. I was left to clean the mosque, lock up and do whatever other duties he had left undone.

My mother used to sew and I helped. According to her, my sisters didn't know what they were doing when they helped her, so she preferred my help.

When I enrolled at Bonteheuwel Senior Secondary School, life became very easy. I was always attractive so getting with the 'right crowd' was never a problem. Popularity was always easy for people with looks.

I was a good student in high school and kept doing what I had to do. I was always lost in my books at school and after that I would go straight to *madressa*, go home and then go to mosque for both evening prayers. This was the cycle of my daily routine and it didn't actually bother me. I enjoyed it at the time. I was born into this Muslim family that followed the *deen* to the tee. I was not going to be any different. There were things that were acceptable, and certain things that weren't. There were certain barriers that could not be crossed. This firm foundation that was laid beneath me guided my entire life. It made sure that I followed the 'proper' path.

I had never considered or thought that I was different to most other boys. I thought that I was exactly like them. My teachers, however, knew differently. When I was in my third year of high school, a teacher called me into her classroom. I found not just her there, but two other teachers. I was wondering what was going on, and I soon found out.

'Are you gay, or are you not?' they asked me in unison.

I could see that they were curious and when I asked them why they'd ask this, they replied that it seems like I was different. I just didn't understand it yet because I wasn't really gay. I was transgendered and I had not come to terms with the woman within me yet. I stood there looking at them and some of it kind of slipped into place. It was as if a light bulb lit up; it immediately dawned on me that they were right to a certain extent. They started to explain what this life would entail. They also referred to one of the teachers who was openly gay at my school and he knew what he was talking about.

They highlighted that they understood my predicament because of who my father was and how much more problematic things would become if I chose this lifestyle. I knew what they meant. They were talking about the religious implications that all of this would have on my family and myself. How would father deal with this? Would he be able to understand? I didn't know and wasn't really that worried about it. I also didn't feel like I needed to discuss this with anyone. In any case, I was always in the mosque so I didn't need to speak to anyone else but Allah. If Allah couldn't give me answers, then no one would be able to.

My mother's sewing started to boom, so she began a little home business. I was helping her constantly. I took advantage of this opportunity to create a new image for myself. As she bought new materials, I would make myself a new garment, or my mother would. My schoolmates thought that I was rich. They would constantly see me in different outfits. Some even thought that I was the only child. Where I lived, it was considered rich if you had so much clothing. But my family was never affluent; we were poor. Our riches lay in the things that weren't connected to money.

I was always a positive and assertive person so I would never allow myself to be influenced by others. I was a leader and not a follower, in that way. I was very mature. I think that my maturity stemmed from the lengthy in-depth conversations that I had with the older people at the mosque. After prayers, the men generally lingered and insisted that I join them in their conversations about the religion and sport. I didn't turn them down due to being polite, but I also enjoyed the men's company.

My first really gay relationship was with this boy from school, whose father had been the previous leader at the local mosque. We had become friends because of our backgrounds. We became very close friends. I remember the delight on my dad's face when I told him about the friendship. He had just left the mosque after an argument between himself and someone else. When he heard about the friendship, he was ecstatic. His mood changed instantly. He raved about what a blessing it is to have good friendships, especially if it is with those who come from a similar background. He enjoyed the fact that I was keeping such good company, but if he only knew!

We never got involved sexually, we just kissed and touched and that was all. We were both very nervous about what we were doing because we both came from very staunch Muslim backgrounds. We were taught that Islam condemned this type of behaviour. Sharing these kinds of feelings for each other was forbidden. Hence we were filled with guilt and shame.

This was around my fourth year in high school and I enjoyed myself with him. He used to come around to my house and we would go out together. My parents would be okay with it because he came from very much the same kind of family as ours. We attended *madressa* together in the afternoons and in the evening we would accompany each other home after our evening prayers at the mosque. The relationship between the two of us was becoming very obvious during my last year at school and people started gossiping about it. I think my parents eventually had their suspicions, but never had the nerve to discuss it with either of us. They were too afraid of what the neighbours may think or do. So, they merely pretended that it did not exist and we kept it in hiding.

Now, there came a time when I accepted my sexuality. I felt that I was not accepted in the fold of Islam and hence I started clubbing toward the end of my second-last year in high school. This was the way in which I started to get comfortable with who I was. After all, I was told that Islam does not accept me.

I met Natasha. She introduced me to a few of her gay friends. They were the ones who introduced me to the club scene. On my first visit to the club, I knew that I would become a regular club-goer. I was fascinated to see so many people who were free and at peace. They accepted themselves and were extremely friendly. Some wore dresses and were very comfortable within themselves. I was surprised that the guilt and shame just left me. There were other people like me! I immediately decided to return dressed as a woman, so that all questions could be cleared.

My clubbing took over most of my life during these stages and I went as a woman because then people knew exactly where I stood and because I liked it too. I would go to the club as a drag queen and I would enjoy the world of being a woman with a short skirt and revealing clothing. Then I would change at a friend's place before I went back home, where I would be a Muslim boy again. I was only a drag queen on the weekends and I loved the double life that I was living because it was so much fun. I always wondered what was going to happen to me with regard to my religion. I always wondered what would become of me once I passed on. *Some people told me I was doomed to hell.* I am a very happy person but there was the worrying side that spoke within me. Whenever I would go clubbing then I'd wonder all about religion. Today I no longer see myself as a drag queen, but rather as a woman in a man's body.

It was very difficult to learn this new language and culture, but eventually, as always, I mastered it. My new life had begun! I was now a woman! Ever since that day, I always wore women's clothing. It felt natural. But I had to do it secretively.

Intimate relationships were difficult because I didn't know where I was yet. I could also no longer continue my relationship with my best friend because he was not interested in my new lifestyle. I believed that if I was going to be in a relationship, then I did not want to hide it from anyone. I needed someone who could publicly acknowledge that we were dating. I wanted someone who would walk proudly into a club with me. All the guys who were prepared to do this always became jealous. They wanted me to look good for them alone. They would get angry if I would spend time with other people. I've never understood this. It was always the same thing and thus my relationships never really lasted very long.

It was only at the age of twenty that my parents eventually confronted me about my sexuality and dress code. They gave me an ultimatum. I needed to change or leave, and I chose to leave. I moved from my parents' house to my aunt's house, also in Bonteheuwel. She was a gem; although she too was Muslim, she didn't have a problem with the gay community. She was also a dressmaker and she made my clothing and other things that I wore to the club. She did not really condone my clubbing, but she loved me because of who I was. She treated me as family is supposed to be treated. I was always pleased by her attitude towards me especially because my immediate family rejected me. She even introduced me to the song: *I am who I am*. She was never judgemental, she merely loved me completely. She accepted all my gay friends and she has had gay friends of her own. She was true to the religion because she believed that it is not her place as a human being to judge. Maybe that is why she was so popular in the area. She does community work, she goes to mosque and she sews for a lot of people.

I remember my teachers telling me that the gay life is a lonely one, but for me it really hasn't been that way. I've accepted my life and I'm actually enjoying being who I am. The few really painful incidents along the way were never based on my sexuality. For example, there was once a problem where one of my 'girlfriends' was seeing a gangster. One evening at a karaoke, we realised that she was not at the table. Someone mentioned that she may be outside. From the doorway we could see a guy fighting with his girlfriend. When we went closer, we saw it was her. She and her gangster boyfriend were fighting. I stopped the fighting and told him to get off her. He looked at me, and then I hit him. At this point, his friends surrounded me. I just stood my ground until they shoved a gun in my face. I pushed the gun away and I said that if he thinks he's man enough, then he must come and hit me. He just stood there and I moved my friends inside.

During those days I was living in Woodstock, but it wasn't working out. So, for two months, I had to move back to my parents' home in Bonteheuwel, and afterwards to Salt River. It was during this time that I sat and reflected on my life. I wondered why there were so many negative things happening in my life. I realised that all these things only happened to me when I was with the wrong types of friends. I vowed that I would choose better friends and break my relationships with the ones I had.

I pause as I look at the interviewer. For a moment I forgot that he was there. Then I slowly asked him: 'I wonder why my aunt accepted my sexuality, but my mother and father could not? What was the reasoning behind all this and why was it so complicated? What made it complicated? Is it the people? Is it the Quran?'

Before he could answer my questions I responded by saying that it cannot be the Quran because it is people who read and misinterpret it.

So, I know that I am merely what I am because I was born this way. I was always strong in my belief, and I never faltered. I may have become a bit lenient in my responsibilities, but I never doubted my God. I knew that God was always with me and will remain with me up until the end. I have realised that faith has nothing to do with people's perceptions of doing right or wrong. It is not for people to pass judgement. God will judge based on my beliefs and my connection with Allah, whom is divine.

10

Finding love

'Happy birthday,' my grandmother says as she walks in with my birthday cake. She passes my mother who has finally gotten used to me being with a woman. My other family members all stand around looking at me. Some look at me with hate, some with disdain, and some with genuine acceptance. I appreciate those who support me and no longer feel the negative energy from those who don't. I wasn't always like this and my mother didn't always accept me. But let me start at the beginning...

The Muslim community in Cape Town generally has a very customary Islamic view and practice. They trust what they learn from the *ulema* instead the Quranic scripture. This is based on the Muslim community originating from slaves captured from various parts of the world and keeping their faith alive through an oral tradition. Also, very few people speak and understand Arabic, which is the language in which the Quran was written.

My family was a typically conventional Muslim one. Homosexuality was never spoken about and, if it did come up in conversation, it was under the pretext that 'those people' were going to burn in hell. My parents made sure that we understood that being gay meant an abomination, a condemnation that is definitely not Allah's will. The image was burnt into our minds so that it would remain vivid. When we spoke about gay people, it was never about anyone we knew. We severed all ties with people who announced that they were gay. From a young age already, I questioned most of the things I was taught and I didn't feel that everything could work in the manner that was described by my family. I had accepted some of what my parents and teachers told me, but I would always ask questions in an effort to get a better understanding.

At a young age I realised that I was different from other girls and that I saw girls in a different way. I liked playing with girls, but there was something about my fondness that I didn't understand well enough. I thought about it because that was how I worked things out. I realised that this was what my parents were talking about and what they dreaded and hated. I suppressed my emotions from then on because of my upbringing and what I was taught. I didn't feel like anything was wrong with me and I didn't feel bad about it. I posed carefully structured questions to my mother and say little things that caught their attention, and they would say that *shaytan* was busy with me. I thus became hesitant to tell people about my sexuality because I feared that they would have negative reactions towards me. I didn't feel like the devil was having an adverse effect on my life. I felt normal and that was all that mattered for now.

Throughout my teenage years, I dated boys to keep everyone away from me. It was also a coping mechanism to suppress my feelings. I couldn't allow myself to entertain the thought of being with a woman, at least not until much later when I got to a turning point in my life. My family encouraged my relationships with these 'boyfriends' because they felt that a woman is second to a man. They believed that in order to fulfil her role and obligations to society that a woman must get married to a man and be subservient to him. She should also, once married, move into his household. This never made sense to me. I don't say this as a criticism of Islamic beliefs, but from my point of view, as an individual. I believe that all people are born equal to each other. But my parents would hear none of this. They went on and on about how I should be like other girls in the community and not question my religion and fate.

I pretended not to care about what they said about me and how I should live my life. I was becoming frustrated because of all the remarks I was getting from family and friends. I didn't see why I needed to fit into a society that refuses to accept me for who I am. I was constantly defending my beliefs and one day after I had a fall out with my mom's friend, I decided that it was time to come clean. I was tired of the pretence, the suppression and the frustration! Why was I hiding it anyway? I was nineteen and done with school. I was an adult and I decided it was time to tell my family about my attraction to women.

I wrote them a two-page letter describing the way I felt and how I detested living a lie. I told them that I was a lesbian and that I wanted to date girls. I was tired of hiding who I was and I didn't want to lose them, but this was something that I needed to do. I just kept harping on how sorry I was and that I understood the impact it would have on them. I told them that I was sorry for being the way I am, but explained that I was born this way.

I packed my bags and basically ran away from home. I went to a friend's house. For the one day that I was there, all I could think of was what my parents were going to do. I decided to ready myself for the worst. I figured that they were going to disown me. Unfortunately for me though, that's not what they did.

What they did was much worse! I couldn't believe that my parents could do something like that to me. They came to fetch me from my friend's place and then brought me back home. I was locked in my room. I had to stay there until I changed. I couldn't believe what was taking place. They took my phone, and hid all other forms of communication from me. All the keys were kept from me, and I wasn't allowed to see or talk to anyone. I was stuck in my room. The same room that used to be my sanctuary became my prison cell.

One day my parents waltzed in and told me that I was going out with them. I wasn't allowed to talk to anyone and I wasn't allowed to wander away from them. They took me to a Muslim organisation for therapy. When we got there, I started reading the notice boards to see what happened here. As I looked around I saw an article about a learned man from the clergy who had come to the organisation to discuss homosexuality. He had different views and ideas from the mainstream Muslim community. He even substantiated his views with Quranic scripture. I felt my heart lifting a bit, but it was not for long. When we were finally called into the consultation room, my mother led the way, I was in the middle, and my dad was the last to enter the room. He closed the door behind him. We then sat down and I noticed that the councillor had a huge pile of files before her and she seemed very agitated. It looked like she had so many other things to do. The councillor barely had a chance to greet us because my mother started ranting and raving. She was shouting like a mad person and said: 'My daughter's a lesbian and she's not supposed to be this way.'

The councillor just looked at her incredulously and sighed heavily. She looked like she needed a bit of sleep. As we sat waiting for her reply, I prepared myself for the worst. She then turned to look at all of us, as she rubbed her eyes.

She said to my mom, 'I can't change your daughter. She is the way she is and you should accept it. There are parents out there who have bigger problems with their children. I can't fix something that isn't broken.'

There was a silence before she concluded, 'Remember, being gay is not a disease, it isn't contagious, it's a part of who people are.'

My mother went crazy and stormed out of there with me behind her. For the time being I went back to being locked in a room.

One thing I have noticed about our society was its hypocrisy about *Hadith*. I personally would like to know which ones we follow and which we disregard? For example, my family had a problem with me moving out of the house without getting married. They said that there is a *Hadith* that decrees that a woman is supposed to move from her father's house into her husband's house. But is this really so? These are some of the questions that I pondered while I was stuck in that room. My family would come to me in groups and would hammer at me with their versions of the truth. They would tell me about what the Quran professed without producing any proof. I had to sit there and listen to all this; I couldn't do anything about it because I was completely defenceless. They broke down my self-esteem, making me lose my sense of pride and self-worth. I felt degraded and dejected. I went through so many things that caused emotional damage. Eventually I decided to play 'straight' again, just to free myself from their torture.

I couldn't understand why everyone around me wanted to tell me what I should do. I knew what would make me happy! All I needed to make myself happy, at this stage, was to be left alone. I knew what was best for me and I tried to relay this to them. They just didn't want to see my point of view. They repeatedly told me that I was possessed by the devil. My one grandfather even told me that I was possessed by many demons. I brushed it off because I didn't want any further arguments.

I was forced back into the closet in exchange for my freedom. What they didn't know, was that I was still dating women. I couldn't deny who I was. I found it hard to believe that this God whom I serve, and Someone who loves me so much, was going to completely disregard everything I've ever done in my life, based on who I love. I wasn't hurting anyone. I was bringing love, comfort, warmth and peace to someone else, and I couldn't see how this could possibly be wrong. The love shared between the two of us could not possibly be wrong. There was no justification that it could be wrong. My family must be confused because all religions speak of love as being a righteous thing, and not a wicked one. I continued dating women in secret. I felt that if I got caught and locked up again, at least I would have had a few happy experiences.

A few years later I met an amazing girl called Stacy. I fell completely in love with her. She was smart, funny and attractive and she loved me too. I felt that I had found the girl whom I was supposed to be with. I couldn't live with the lies anymore.

It was eating at my soul and it left me barren and hurt. I became physically sick because I was lying everyday to these people whom I was supposed to love the most. I again moved out of my parents' home. They didn't do anything this time because I was now an adult and had the final say when it came to my life. I shared an apartment with my girlfriend and they did not know where it was. I sent them a lengthy telephone text message. I told them the way I felt and why I moved out.

For a long time I didn't hear from my parents. In fact the very first time I heard from my mother again was just after my parents got divorced. She called me. She said that she wanted me to be with her during this difficult period in her life. She said that she would really appreciate me to be with her, rather than anyone else.

'No one else' were her words. It was strange for me because here my mother was depending on me. I could never depend on her. She never wanted to speak with me, but now she was seeking solace from me. This act is what cemented our relationship. Our bond grew stronger as I sustained her emotional well-being.

Today my mom threw a party and celebrated her lesbian-in-the-family's birthday. Despite having her reservations about my relationship with Stacy, she has made every effort to get to know her. Soon I became very close to my dad. Currently I continue to spend weekends at his place. Both my parents also stop by from time to time.

I look back and it hasn't been such a bad life. The lessons I learnt from my ocean of experiences moulded me into the person I am today. Allah made me this way because there was the knowledge that I could handle it. He knew it would make me a better and stronger person.

I believe that this is why everyone goes through trials in life. Allah provides us with a test in order to appreciate life.

11

Trials in love

A little boy ran across the dirt path and fell on the other side of the road. He looked at his scraped knees as the pain registered. Blood ran freely from the open wounds, and he jumped up and limped over to the barn where his dad was. He had cried all the way to the barn and, as he entered the barn, he was quickly smacked. He fell on his back again, and then stifled his tears.

'Stop crying, you sissy!' his father shouted and feigned another blow, throwing the boy back on to the floor as he was trying to stand up. With his back against the ground, the boy grew angry, and coughed as the dust gathered around him. He stood up and looked his father in his eyes. 'I hate you and one day I'm going to leave here.'

He then ran to the house to complain to his mother. She soothed him, plastered the cut and dried his tears.

He kept his promise to his father. He had barely turned eighteen when he told his dad he was taking the truck and leaving. He didn't care where he was headed and he wasn't concerned about how he would get money on the other side. All he knew was that he needed to get away from his father because he felt sick staying on this farm with him. His father watched as he pulled out of the driveway not bothering to even say goodbye to his only son. He knew there were some peculiarities with his son, but he did not wish to investigate it. He just watched his son leave and then continued with his work on the farm.

Yusuf sat in the truck and was unaffected by the fact that his father and mother had not come to bid him farewell. The night before; he had told them that he was leaving, and they both just looked at him as if he were confused.

'Why now?' they asked. 'What's wrong with you?' All he did was look at his father, because he knew his father was very aware of why he wanted to leave, he just refused to accept it.

He looked in the rear-view mirror for the last time and watched as his home faded into oblivion. He started to feel the loss within him, but he kept it bottled inside.

'I'm not sorry I left them,' he told himself, 'things were never going to work out for me there.' He could feel the tears start to roll down his cheeks, but he ignored it.

He made himself forget about the good things he was leaving behind, and concentrated on what he was going to do when he reached his destination. The evening quickly rolled in to night and he was starting to feel the drain of travelling alone. He looked out ahead and all he could see was darkness. There was no way of seeing more than ten metres ahead because his headlights were the only source of light on this highway. He dug into his bag and got out something to keep himself awake and looked back through the windshield as he ate. He looked at the dark expanse before him, and started hating it because his mind kept drifting back to his family. He kept thinking about how he left them, and what he could have done instead, but then would realise that there was nothing else to do. His father had always treated him in the same way he treated his farm animals, brutally. He turned on the radio to drown out his thoughts, but a few minutes after switching it on, it fizzled and the signal died. So he sat there looking at this ocean of black oil before him, and listening to static within the car and he found it kind of soothing. The monotony of the static and the unchanging landscape made him feel as if he was in a movie, and he was losing himself. He lost track of the time as he drove and was surprised as the sun began to rise on the horizon. The city came into view after a few minutes, and although it was still a distance away, the fact that he could see it made all the difference.

As he drove into the city, he looked for somewhere to eat, and found one in the corner at the petrol station. He sat down and started thinking about what he was going to do now that he was here.

He only had a R100 bill in his pocket which he got from his neighbours for helping with their house, a row of shoes which were stowed behind the seat he was sitting on and a few clothes in his bag in the truck. The waitress came and took his order and, as he waited he grabbed some of the newspapers on the rack to start job hunting. He became so engrossed with looking for work that he barely noticed the waitress return with his coffee and sandwich. He also failed to notice someone sitting down opposite him.

He stopped to take a sip of his coffee and noticed the stranger.

'New here?' he asked. Yusuf surveyed him and calculated whether he could talk to this person. He looked fairly decent so he decided it was alright.

'Yes,' he said, 'I just got in from farm country and I am looking for work and a place to stay.'

'Any luck so far?' he asked, as he took a sip of his own coffee.

'None,' Yusuf replied. 'But I never really expected there to be any work for a farm boy in the city.'

'You should try the retail stores.' The stranger said. 'They are always looking for new people and you are attractive enough for them to hire.'

Yusuf sat and thought to himself: about the retail work, about this stranger's suggestions and the fact that he thinks that he's attractive.

'Thanks.' Yusuf decided if he was a bad person, it would have shown by now. 'I'm Yusuf.'

'Frederick,' he said, and took Yusuf's hand in his own.

In that moment Yusuf knew Frederick was like him. He didn't find Frederick attractive in that sense, but he knew that Frederick was meant to be his first friend in the city. They finished their coffee and Frederick offered to help him with his CV, and he was soon up and about searching for work. He soon received a call to Frederick's number saying that he had an interview with Edgars on Monday, and he started feeling excited. He had spent two weeks of staying in his truck, and washing at baths and now finally he was getting a break into the working world. It was Thursday and Frederick thought that they should celebrate this interview, so planned to go out the Friday night.

In this time, Yusuf had made another friend, but this one he was dating. Sieraaj still stayed with his parents, but they knew about him and his relations with other men. He also had a younger sister but he was very selective about what he told her. Yusuf was invited to them on Sunday for lunch and so he was planning on enjoying the weekend.

Friday night finally came and Yusuf and Frederick parked the truck. They went in and came out at about one o'clock, and headed toward the truck; only to find that it was not there. Yusuf thought about it for a second, and then burst out laughing and couldn't believe he hadn't thought of this happening. Frederick, being the good-hearted person that he was, started running down the hill to see if it hadn't rolled down. This made Yusuf convulse with laughter, and he spent the next half hour trying to regain control of himself. Once he did, he started worrying about the fact that all his shoes were still in that truck so all he had now were his clothes, which were at Frederick's house, and the R100 which was still in his pocket.

He was then forced to lend shoes from Frederick to go to his boyfriend's house for Sunday lunch and for the interview on Monday. The lunch with Sieraaj and his parents went swimmingly and although they were a bit abrupt and apprehensive, Yusuf kept himself under control, because this was just about meeting the parents. Yusuf got on well with Sieraaj's baby sister, Zahra, who was very energetic and very sweet. He left that house with a sense of contentment. After Sieraaj dropped him at Frederick's place, they kissed and it was the perfect end to a great day.

The following morning he went to the interview and he went in very confident, as he knew why he was doing this. He left there at one o'clock. At one-thirty they called him to tell him that the job was his. He smiled widely as he was glad for the job. He got home and told Frederick about it, and Frederick said that he could then move in with him now that he could pay the rent. Yusuf started working and found he was really interested in the clothing industry. It kept him busy and so he stuck with it. Any opportunities that arose, he jumped at and he grew in the industry.

Through all this, he dated Sieraaj and they made the most of this relationship. They both had strong feelings for each other and they wanted the relationship. Yusuf was offered the opportunity to move on to another company that offered him more money.

He might have started off a farm boy, but he quickly learnt how things worked in the city and everything just fell into place. It wasn't that different to the world he had lived in, and so all it really took was a shift in thinking. He knew where he should go and what he should do in order to get ahead in this world. He wasn't afraid of all the new challenges. When they had enough money, Yusuf and Sieraaj invested in a house, and they moved in together. This did not keep Yusuf from excelling in his work. He wasn't expecting to grow so fast. He couldn't believe his luck at the beautiful bond that he shared with Sieraaj.

It went well for a very long time, until an earth shattering moment. One day he came back from work and found that Sieraaj was not home yet. He called him, and someone else picked up his mobile phone. He put the receiver down and sat down, with his eyes glued to the phone, thinking about the voice he had just heard. *Who was it?* he asked himself as he watched the phone.

He sat in that same position for the rest of the day, debating who the other person could possibly have been. He knew he was losing it as he sat there talking to himself and waiting for Sieraaj to come home.

Sieraaj eventually walked through the front door. Yusuf was waiting for him as he entered the front room. Sieraaj stopped in his tracks. His face was contorted with pain. It was evident he was uncomfortable and would rather be somewhere else. He took a step back, but Yusuf fixed him with a glare that kept him in place.

'Where were you?' Yusuf asked. He waited a few minutes for a reply as Sieraaj slowly put down his bag and took a seat opposite Yusuf.

'*As-salaamu alaikum,*' Sieraaj said to Yusuf. It came out very unnatural.

'*Wa alaikum salaam,*' Yusuf replied snidely. 'Where were you this afternoon?'

'At work,' he replied.

'At work?' Yusuf said, his tone rising a bit. 'I called work, and they said you weren't there and when I called your cell, someone else picked up.'

Sieraaj sat there, not saying a word. He just looked at Yusuf who was looking at him wide eyed.

'Who was that who answered your phone?' He asked. 'Where were you?'

Sieraaj stayed silent, and watched as Yusuf grew angrier and angrier. It was difficult to read what Sieraaj was thinking as he kept his face in a plain expression.

'Is this going to happen all the time?' He asked. 'How long has this been going on?'

Yusuf's temper was growing as Sieraaj refused to answer, but he was trying to keep it under control. Sieraaj didn't defend himself. He just remained silent. This infuriated Yusuf even more.

'SPEAK TO ME!' Yusuf shouted, tears suddenly welling up within him.

For the first time he thought about how he felt about Sieraaj.

He knew he loved him and couldn't bear the thought of not being with him. He felt his heart convulse and start to race as he considered it more and more. He stopped himself and thought logically about it all.

'I can't stay if this is going to continue,' he said, and when Sieraaj stayed quiet, he stood up and headed to the room, and started gathering up his things.

A moment later, Sieraaj followed Yusuf into the room and wrapped his arms around him. 'Don't go.'

Yusuf tried to fight against his embrace, but failed terribly. He started shouting at Sieraaj, but Sieraaj just wouldn't let go. He kept kissing Yusuf and his embrace just seemed to grow tighter by the minute, as if he didn't want to lose Yusuf.

'I love you, please don't go!' he repeated. His voice crackled with desperation and the last word came out in a whisper. Yusuf could hear the conviction in his words, but he knew that it didn't make a difference. He couldn't let this affect him.

'How can you love me when you're sleeping with someone else?' Yusuf shouted, finally breaking away from Sieraaj.

'It's not something I can explain to you,' Sieraaj said, hoping to end the conversation, but he knew it couldn't end there.

'Then I need to leave,' Yusuf said. 'If you can't tell me what it is, how can I make it better? You can't be with me and someone else at the same time!' Yusuf screamed and grabbed what he could and headed out. He slammed the door and drove to Frederick's house. Frederick knew he was coming. He immediately went to the guest bedroom and cried for hours on end. He didn't care what was happening around him, he just sat there and cried. He lost himself in his tears and sat there, thinking about how his father had always said he shouldn't.

He shut his father's face out, as he worked at clearing his mind. He tried to shut out everything, but all it was driving him crazy.

He stayed with Frederick a few days, but soon found himself another flat of his own. He began to lose himself in his work and soon received better career opportunities from other companies.

'That's not going to help you,' Frederick said one night, 'he'll still be in your head.'

'I can deal with that,' Yusuf said, 'I just can't deal with possibly bumping into him on a daily basis.'

With that he moved again, leaving behind this city that he had grown to love and take as his new home. Love was not as simple as he thought it would be. He also thought that love between two men would be easier, but he was mistaken.

He started working for another retail company and they supplied him with a car, a place to stay and money to travel. He was hired as a fashion buyer. He would have to find trends and buy the clothes that he thought would sell. He loved this job, because he liked fashion, but also because it helped him better himself in an entrepreneurial sense. He quickly learnt how to get things done, and was one of the 'high buyers' after a few months.

He found his next threshold in life by sheer coincidence. He needed a stapler for a presentation he was doing and he sent his assistant to purchase it. There were no shops in the mall that sold staplers. 'That's weird,' Yusuf said, without giving it much thought. When he got home, he thought about it and realised that this would be the perfect niche to invest in. If he had enough money, then he could start his own stationery business. That's just what he did. He left his job at the retail store and found himself a vacant space in the mall and opened up his small business. He started off small, but was proud for finally doing something on his own.

He had been dating a few guys on and off, but none as serious as Sieraaj. There were nights when past memories of Sieraaj came back to haunt him, but he was quick to jump into his work to forget about it.

Years passed very easily then, and he soon found himself reaching thirty-five. He was still riveted to the memory of Sieraaj.

He could not move forward with any intimate relationships. When he looked in the mirror, there was Sieraaj. When he crossed the street, he saw Sieraaj. When he slept Sieraaj was in every dream. He was reluctant to admit it, but he was fixated with Sieraaj. He couldn't forget him at all. Eventually he decided to put the ghosts to rest. He called Sieraaj on his old number. It rang four times before someone picked it up.

'Hello?' a voice said on the other side.

'Hello, Sieraaj?' Yusuf asked hesitantly into the phone.

'He's in the shower,' the voice said. 'Can I ask him to call y–'

Yusuf hung up the phone before the other person could finish speaking. He sat on the bed breathing deeply.

'Why did I do that?' he asked himself, close to the edge again. He jumped from the bed, hopped in front of the computer and concentrated on work again.

He stayed in this state for a week before Frederick landed on his doorstep. Yusuf had completely forgotten about Frederick coming to visit. He quickly recovered though, and put on his public face, but Frederick could sense that something was wrong.

'What's going on?' he asked as they sat watching television.

'What do you mean?' Yusuf asked, dumbfounded, 'the TV is fine.'

'I mean with you?' he replied, 'I haven't seen you like this since the day you left Sieraaj. Please don't tell me you still haven't gotten over him.'

Yusuf already knew it was useless arguing with Frederick, so he didn't even try to deny his feelings.

'I can't let him go,' he said simply. 'I called him last week and some guy picked up the phone.'

'So what did you do?' Frederick asked.

'Nothing,' Yusuf replied, 'I just put down the phone and went on working.'

'That's your solution for everything, isn't it?' Frederick said, his voice rising slightly.

'What do you know?' Yusuf said loudly, 'you've never felt what I feel for Sieraaj. You've never had to go through the kind of pain I had to endure.' Yusuf fumed and walked briskly from the room as the doorbell rang. He composed himself before answering the door. He pulled it open and nearly fainted in shock.

Sieraaj stood in the doorway, as if an apparition had just appeared to replace what he wished would happen. He stood there for a moment taking in the spectacle before him. Sieraaj hadn't changed, or at least as far as he could see there was no change.

'Sieraaj?' Yusuf stammered in disbelief.

'Who's at the door?' Frederick called from behind him.

'*Salaam* Frederick,' Sieraaj said, and smiled at Frederick through the gate.

'Speak about the devil and he shall come scratching at your door,' Frederick said, and then headed back inside.

'Can I come in?' Sieraaj asked, while Yusuf stood transfixed by him.

'Yusuf?' Sieraaj stood outside waiting until Yusuf finally snapped out of his reverie. He opened the gate and walked back in, and Sieraaj followed him slowly. The first thing they saw as they entered the house was Frederick sitting comfortably on the couch. Yusuf went over to the kitchen counter and stood behind it, while Sieraaj stood awkwardly by the entrance to the dining room.

'What do you want?' Frederick asked Sieraaj coldly, in an attempt to protect his friend.

Sieraaj was about to reply, but Yusuf was too fast and jumped at the opportunity first.

'I appreciate what you're doing Frederick, but I need to handle this on my own, and there are certain things Sieraaj and I need to discuss alone, if you don't mind,' Yusuf said as he walked from the kitchen and handing Sieraaj a cup of tea. He looked at Frederick and when he returned from the kitchen with his own tea cup, Frederick was gone.

Yusuf sat anxiously across from Sieraaj, waiting to hear what he wanted to say.

'What are you doing here, Sieraaj?' Yusuf asked, and then took a sip of his tea.

The room was silent as the two sat watching each other. Clearly this is not what he had expected to happen. His face depicted a deep disappointment, and for a moment Yusuf wanted to cure that disappointment, but changed his mind.

'Well, you called me, and when Ishma'el picked up, you hung up.' He stopped, took a sip of his tea, and then continued. 'I've loved you ever since the very beginning and I always have, but there are just certain things I cannot expect you to do for me.'

'So you're finally going to tell me why you needed to sleep with other people?' Yusuf sat up expectantly.

'I'd prefer not to, but clearly you make it impossible to refuse.' He said. 'I'm into some really weird stuff, sexually, Yusi.' His spine tingled as Sieraaj used his pet name, which he hadn't heard since last they were together. 'I can't expect you to do those things for me, and I feel embarrassed that I need those things. 'That's why I couldn't talk to you about it.' He stopped, breathing a bit faster now, and trying to contain himself. He explained it all in detail and Yusuf was completely surprised by what he said. He couldn't believe that Sieraaj could want all these things that he definitely couldn't do. Some of it was just too repulsive to him. That was why Sieraaj hadn't told him anything about it.

As he sat there, one thing became very clear to him: He needed to ask himself just how much he loves Sieraaj? Was it enough to let him fulfil his sexual desires with other people? This was definitely not an option. He couldn't put himself through such humiliation for the sake of love. He just couldn't compromise on that. However, it felt natural for him to want Sieraaj to be happy, and the only way he was going to be happy was to let him have these encounters with other people. He knew that he couldn't live without Sieraaj and yet he couldn't allow him to play out his sexual fantasies with others. He was in a dilemma. He wasn't sure what to do, but his automatic response was to stand up, go to him and kiss him. 'Let us work on our issues and needs together. Together with Allah we can make it work.'

And in that one moment, he finally felt free from the burden of being without Sieraaj. He finally felt home and he could feel the love emanating from Sieraaj toward him. Everything felt right and he knew that he would have to deal with Sieraaj. But now he knew that Sieraaj loved him. That was good enough for now. He knew that he couldn't live without Sieraaj any longer, everything was suddenly balanced.

They embraced passionately.

They still live together.

12

This is reality

'Hey *moffie*!' The words keep ringing in my ears. 'How are you going to survive?' The question haunts me to this very day. I guess it's part of the fear and challenges faced by a queer in denial; growing up in the ghetto; the heart of persecution, in Cape Town. Knowing that my thoughts and feelings were not the same as other boys' confused me. I used to feel worried, scared and sad all at the same time.

The voices of reason kept telling me that it was not right. These feelings I feel, these ideas I have, this lifestyle I imagine is not right. It is not acceptable to the people around me, and therefore I have to conform and fall in line with what they say. I have to be rough and rude; I have to be careless and rigid. That is not me.

I stood there thinking about this and then Peter, the school's star athlete, brushed against me as I he headed to the showers. His loose track pants swinging from side to side around the legs and showing everything that I shouldn't be seeing. His sweaty body smelt sweet and sent signals to the erotic regions of my body, as he leant over me to grab his towel from behind me. I didn't yet understand what these signals meant and why I was feeling this way for a boy, but it felt right to me. This accidental moment made me think about and realise that I liked boys and not girls. I started worrying as I stood there and heard the shower go on behind me. I was scared of what this all would mean in the future and how I couldn't map out anything now because I didn't know anyone like this.

Ok, let's just take a step back, as I kind of got ahead of myself.

Now I need to warn you that I wish no pity or sympathy to cross your mind. I just want that you learn from this story; that you realise that you're not alone in what you're going through; that there are many more people that have suffered and are suffering as you are now; or you can take from this story and see the struggles I had endured and save your child, sibling, friend this kind of pain.

I believed that good things happen to good people but now I'm not so sure. For example, my grandfather was a good person but then one day he died of AIDS, and everyone was shocked. He was loved by all in the neighbourhood and everyone thought he was faithful, but how did he then contract the disease? This was a topic of much discussion in the time that followed his death and it made me realise that people would quickly change their perception of you when they hear something new. It sickened me to think that these people, who were supposedly my grandfather's friends, would speak of him like this. My mother started losing her grip on the world and she started getting worried about herself so sent me to live with my dad. This completely turned my world upside down as I now had to adjust to his family and his rules. I've never really spent much time with my dad. I only saw him when he would come and drop the maintenance cheque at the house. Now I had to live with him!

I found out that he lived with his parents and had his own family as well: a wife and two children, one boy and one girl. I was barely there a day and I was already given commands to do this and that, watch the children, clean there, do this, do that… I felt like Cinderella, except that no prince was going to save me from this nightmare. I even had to sit and watch everyone play happy family with the children, just in case someone needed something, or an accident happens, then I would be there to take care of it. I never really thought about anything else because I had to concentrate on doing the floors and making sure that everything was in tip-top shape when my dad came home. We never really had a decent conversation. The most he offered me was broken phrases or words lost in oblivion as he passed me. He was always too tired to talk to me, or just needed to do something else, but never returned. That was every week's story, and on the weekend, I learnt that it was always good to put extra padding under my clothes. He would come in at 4:55 religiously, and start beating me for no reason. He would swear at me, he would jerk me around and he would beat me with his belt, a chord, a broom or anything he could lay his hands on. I couldn't sleep for days because of the cuts on my back. I would not be allowed to go to the hospital or report anything to the nurse's office for fear of being beating to just an inch from death. It was a promise my dad made while he was sober and in control of himself. I would never forget that day he looked me in the eyes and just said; 'I'll kill you if you try anything. You speak to anyone, you tell them anything, in any way, and I'll beat you to an inch of your life, and then I'll throw you out to die in the streets. You will regret it!'

He said the last part through gritted teeth and watched what I would do. Naturally, I did nothing as I was merely thirteen years old. I knew the pay-off of disobeying my father, especially when he was threatened. The beatings became common practice and the pain was reduced; it hurt less and less. I became a punching bag for his insecurities. My stepmother was helpless. My mother was pathetic and didn't try to communicate in any way, so all I was doing was going to school, and coming back, as I wasn't allowed a social life. My security was to read The Quran and follow my Muslim practices.

One day I came home a little late from school and my stepmother still expected me to make the food and clean the house. I told her I couldn't do so because I have had too much homework. She went completely ballistic and I was punished by being locked in the storage cupboard with no lights, no food, no water and only the rats to keep me company. This depicts the life I lived for two years until I turned fourteen.

During this period my sexuality started to develop. It was

prominent in the way that I spoke that I was effeminate. This drew a lot of name calling. I felt scandalised and I went to sleep in the evening with tears in my eyes. My dad did nothing to defend me from his family's torrid remarks. They hurt me in the way that no one else can. If your family hurts you, then it hurts more than friends or other people.

That year, my birthday was the worst it ever was or ever will be, without a doubt. My sexuality was realised. I had no cake, no party, no friends invited over. That night my father sent me to the shop. It was already dark and there was a sinister chill in the air. On my way I crossed a field and I walked directly into a trap. A group of gangsters were sitting in the park which was on my side of the field. I pretended that I didn't see them because if I tried to turn and run, they would pounce on me. As I walked forward they called me names. They were kids from the neighbourhood, but because I never got to leave the house, I didn't recognise them. The darkness of the night didn't help either. I started walking faster as I saw them from the corner of my eye. They were approaching very fast. I ran, but before I had run the length of the field, I was tripped from behind. I went skidding across the wet grass. I could feel the dew soak through my pants. I felt my leg throb under the pressure of something being broken. I struggled to get up, but was grabbed by my cuff and held up by one of the guys.

I didn't think that there was any point in resisting. They knew I had money. 'Please…' I pleaded, 'please just take the money… just leave me alone…'

I reached for the money from my pocket to give it to them, but one of them stepped on my hand, breaking the knuckles in three places. I screamed! One of them kicked me in the stomach to kill the scream. I lay there, making *duah*. 'Please Allah allow me to live through this ordeal,' I pleaded. I cannot recall where I got the strength to pray as they kicked and beat me. I tried to cut myself off from the pain. Every time they lashed out at me, it sent a shock through my body. I wasn't able to take any more. I tried crawling away from them, but every time they would just pull me back. They grabbed my hair and dragged me toward the middle of the field again. They rolled me around checking what was in my pockets, emptying them and taking whatever they wanted.

They became bored of beating me and one of them retorted: 'And now we'll see what kind of a *moffie* you are.'

They laughed and jeered. In an instant it dawned on me. I realised their next move. I panicked and started screaming again. One of them retaliated by kicking me in the face, as others spat across my face and tugged at my clothing. My throat swelled. I coughed and splattered blood everywhere. They pushed me down from all sides. I lie naked on the dew drenched grass as they took turns with me. Someone sodomised me and enjoyed every moment of my pain. I lay there struggling as the world looked down upon my perplexed figure. The shop was in sight, but no one seemed to care. I felt the penetration of a second person. I wanted to scream at the pain, but my throat was hoarse. All I could do was moan and groan. By the time I was entered for a third time, the cold had numbed my entire body. My body was still pinned down, even though I could not resist anymore. I faintly heard them cheering each other on. I prayed for some kind of miracle to stop this.

As I forced my face into another direction to stop mud from entering my eyes, I saw a woman and a child walking across the field close by. They froze at the edge of the field as they took in this sight. My blurred vision gave me only a small insight into the two figures standing there. I wanted to plead with them.

HELP ME! I wanted to shout, but I couldn't. All I could do was accept their abandonment as they swiftly turned and sped out of eyeshot. I accepted my fate on that field that day and knew that the persecution and attacks would never stop. I had lost count of how many times I had been violated. I knew that the tears flowing from my eyes went unnoticed as it quickly mixed with the mud forced onto my face. I was sent to a world of oblivion until I realised that everything was finally over. I became conscious of an occasional car passing by. I felt sore and broken. My body ached and it felt as if every bone in my body was broken, it could not move in the way that it should. I forced myself to get up from the ground and hoped that it would get better as I moved on, but it didn't.

The walk home took twice as long as usual. When I finally reached there, I felt dizzy from the blood dripping down my leg. As I opened the door, my dad stood there and scolded at me.

'What the bloody hell took you so long? Why didn't you put on proper clothes to go to the shop? What kept you?'

Not a single word was said about the blood running down my leg, or about my decrepit and filthy state. Not a word said about my torn pants. My tear-stained and mud-filled face did not warrant a sympathetic question about what happened.

'I… got… rob…' This was all I could get out as I headed for the shower. I went into the bathroom and locked the door behind me. I looked at the door for a second, still not really aware of what I was doing. I felt my feet move towards the shower and I felt my hand reach for the shower. I clumsily yanked everything off and got into the bath. Our shower was built into the bath, so the water instantly dripped out. I turned around and looked at myself in the mirror. I was surprised to see that I was still crying. My face felt sedated. I felt nothing. Everything I did was involuntary. My vision was still blurry and I couldn't make out much of what I was seeing, but the tears were obvious. I turned into the steaming water that flowed freely from the head of the shower. I washed every bit of my body. I felt like filth! I scrubbed and scrubbed, but couldn't rid myself from that sense of being dirty. No matter how I tried, nothing seemed to cleanse my body. I was frantic!

Feeling crept slowly back into my limbs I almost wished that it hadn't. The pain came back instantly. I buckled in the bath, falling backward. I lay there, unable to move, unable to speak and not wanting to accept that this happened. Somewhere, as in a distance, I heard my dad shouting about the water bill. The water and the lights were switched off. I wasn't bothered by any of these things. I merely questioned Allah for putting me through this kind of pain. I could not fathom it. This didn't last for long because I blacked out a few minutes later.

The following morning I woke up feeling the same as I did the night before, although I found myself on the cold, hard tiled floor of the bathroom. The door had been broken open and my clothes were still where I left them the previous night. I lay curled naked on the floor like a dog. I uncurled myself and grabbed my clothing. I refused to put them on and headed to my room where I quickly bagged the blood-drenched garments and threw them in the trash. I locked my door and fell onto my bed. My dad, hearing that I was awake, was there in an instant and demanded to enter. I got up slowly and let him in.

'You need to clean the kitchen,' he said, 'and the laundry needs to be done. The machine is broken so you'll need to wash it by hand.'

I gave him an empty look as he turned and walked away.

'Last night I was–' I screamed at him, but he turned to me and stopped me in my tracks.

'I don't care what happened last night,' he said, 'whatever happened, happened. It's over now. You need to deal with it and move on.' He left, leaving the door open behind him.

With three fractured fingers and a hurting body I started on the family's laundry. I finished everything two hours later, went to my room and locked the door. The following day I did not go to school; I went to the clinic instead. I didn't tell them what really happened because I believed that everyone would just laugh at me. I was sick of having to fight the ridicule of society. There was no one I could confide in, and that drove me crazy.

For several weeks, I had nightmares every night and woke up in a sweaty bed. There was no escape for me from the constant recurring nightmares that I had to deal with them. This experience taught me how to mask my true feelings. I always remember that fateful day.

I started worrying about AIDS and the stories that were told about my grandfather, after his death, regardless of the truth. They told me that the virus is transmitted sexually, so I had to get myself tested. I went to find out everything I could about the HI-virus. I learnt a lot and went for my appointment at the local clinic. I sat in a section of the clinic with a board saying 'AIDS PATIENTS'. Everyone who had AIDS, or who was getting tested for it, had to sit in that section. Diabetic patients sitting on the other side of the room, moved further away from me. I wanted to get up and tell them to go to hell. A woman sat down next to me. I looked at her and I wondered if she too had a scare, or if she had the virus.

'You don't mind if I sit here, do you?' the woman said, and I shook my head.

She smiled a semi-toothless grin and took out a magazine which she finished reading a few moments later.

'What are you here for?' She asked me.

'I'm here to get tested,' I said.

'Oh,' she giggled lightly, and then coughed a bit. 'That's why the grannies on that side are shying away from you?'

I laughed at her candour, but nodded in a knowing way.

She then asked me if I had any knowledge about AIDS and how the test works. She explained the entire process.

I shared my story with her. I realised that ignorance was one of the greatest reasons for people to fear the unknown, including homosexuality. This lady was what I needed to renew my faith in Allah and people. I realised that there must've been a reason why Allah let it happen to me. I guess one day I will discover the reasons for my test. But currently, I still don't know why it happened.

I've learnt to accept my fate. It is a necessary part of what I had to go through to become who Allah wanted me to be.

This is reality...

13

Queer reflection

'Gay people suck!' This is what many people believe. Especially for a person like myself who grew up in a very heteronormative society that prescribed very particular roles and behaviours for men and women.

I am not gay... but my brother is. My family's life has been strongly affected by my brother's lifestyle and I wish to convey what I felt the problems were that arose from his revelation; the issues that the family had to work through and the details of what led up to it. I hope that I can lay out the situation and depict the 'drama' adequately enough for you to see and realise the pain and the belittlement that gay people have to endure for most of their lives, especially during their discovery processes. To be affronted by this kind of attitude and oppression, whilst you are still formulating an opinion of the world, is something that is, to me, unforgivable. The effects on certain people may be permanent and some people kill themselves because they feel they cannot openly announce their sexual orientation to the people they love. I hope this never happens and I hope that families will accept and understand the situation that their children, siblings, aunts, uncles, etcetera are going through in confronting their sexuality. The way that they are is not of their own accord, but what they have been given at birth. I hope you understand what I mean once you read this story of my life with my brother.

There are so many things I don't remember about my life growing up with Muhsin. I was seven when he entered this world and I couldn't even really make a connection with him.

I had hoped that maybe if I gave it some time that we would grow to become great friends, but as the years passed on, things didn't really change. It didn't become better, in fact, it might have become worse. The division between the two of us became certain as he was more interested in crocheting, sewing and helping my mother in the kitchen.

I recall my father telling Muhsin, more than a few times, that he should go play outside and stop acting like a woman. Muhsin clearly did not let this bother him, as he carried on doing what he liked. We even found him once plaiting my mother and sister's hair. I sit now and think that we may not have been the most comforting family because we used to mock him and make fun of him. We called him various nasty nicknames. My mother often called him Tahoera. Aghoeya was another one, after an uncle of ours who was slightly effeminate. The favourite was Abu Nawas, after an Arabic poet who apparently had a fetish for young boys. He did not let these names, or our negative attitudes affect him in any way, and even though we grew tired of the names, we kept using it. After a while it became so common practice that we forgot why we used those names.

Thinking about it now, I begin to appreciate and comprehend the struggles Muhsin had to endure as a young boy, later as a teenager and eventually as an adult. He lived in a world of his own, with no one to turn to when he was grappling with his sexual identity. There was also no support for him to deal with the constant teasing and humiliation. This abuse came not only from the immediate family and school mates, but later also from the rest of the family and the broader community.

Muhsin, as a coping mechanism, then started to develop this very stand-offish and 'I will show you all better' attitude, which might have only alienated him further from everybody. He started distancing himself further from everyone and pushed himself into his studies, ignoring everything else because he wanted to prove to everyone that they were all wrong about him.

Muhsin, as with the rest of my family, has always been pious…
and so we had to be, as our parents were very prestigious in the
community. Our mother was the local Muslim school teacher,
and our father was the local imam, so we had no choice but to
become role models for the family and community. We had to
follow the teachings and beliefs of parents and maintain high
morals and values. There were high expectations of us, and we
were all very well aware of them.

Muhsin soon found that he felt rejected by everyone because
of the name calling and the belittlement. The rejection pushed
him further into the *deen* and he buried himself in his studies. He
applied to an Islamic university in Pakistan in his early twenties
to get away from this rejection. Karachi, Pakistan turned out to
be a good thing for him, and the family was happy he wanted to
further his Islamic studies. The family was ecstatic. I remember
how proud everyone was of Muhsin and about how excellent
he was doing in his studies.

Finally there was going to be someone that was going to
follow in our grandfather's footsteps.

I could see and I felt their relief at this turn of events. I started
to study to become an imam, but did not complete it. I still felt
like my parents hadn't forgiven me, but now there was a beacon
of light. Their attention turned to Muhsin and their hope was
now in him to carry out their dreams. Needless to say, we as a
family came to support Muhsin while he was studying, both
morally and financially.

During his first year of study, Muhsin announced to us his
intention of honouring his Islamic obligation by completing the
remaining fifty per cent of his faith by marrying a girl from our
area whom he was friendly with before he left to study. My
mother was over the moon, and spared no expense flying him
home, getting him married and sending the newlyweds off to
study together in Pakistan. Her parents were a bit worried about
their daughter being in a foreign country with no immediate
family close by to help her. They were afraid that bad things

may happen to her. Muhsin assured them that Pakistan was very safe and that he would be with her always, so she would never be alone.

They left then, a few days after the wedding, to Karachi. She settled quickly into the ways and lifestyle of Pakistan. Initially Muhsin did all the shopping and introduced her to all the good people who have helped and supported him.

It was only while Muhsin was away that he and I started building an actual relationship. He always wrote to me wanting to know about the time that I had studied and wanted advice on certain things. I helped him the best I could, but I was truly just glad that we had finally found a way to connect. From his letters to me, I learnt that they were struggling under the conditions in the country. It was all new to them, especially Fatima who soon became pregnant, but they were handling it very well. He said that although they were coping, he sometimes worried about her. He told me in the letters about two guys in Karachi that he had built very close friendships with. He was spending a great deal of time with them. This worried me, for some reason, it might have been that he was spending time with them instead of his pregnant wife.

In my opinion, it was in that distant land where Muhsin finally discovered his true self. This is where his true sexual identity was realised. He may have experienced the emotions of being gay before that, but I don't think that it was as evident. This brought with it great turmoil as he was not aware that there was a label to describe people like him. He also found that there were other people who were in similar situations. I certainly wasn't aware that people could be attracted to their own sex. I don't know whether that was due to my own naivety, or whether it was because of our very sheltered and strictly religious upbringing. I was never told about people like that in *madressa*, they've never mentioned it to me. Strange as it may seem, I had never encountered anyone who was gay or lesbian at this late stage in my life. I was raised in a neighbourhood consisting of staunch Allah-conscious people, and if anyone was gay there, they probably wouldn't tell. The cost of revelation would definitely have been persecution of some sort by their very own community. I used to wonder about that, but soon just let it go as ignorance.

Around this time, I had very little contact with my family. They had rejected me because of my wayward lifestyle that my very orthodox, opinionated family didn't approve of. I became an outcast. My mother basically told me not to come near her even if something happened to her, or at least until I repented and lived my life the way I was raised.

Thinking about it now, that was definitely the darkest period of my life.

I started questioning the values of my family and their dogmatic interpretation of the religion. As a result I turned my back on both my family and religion. My way of life plus the fact that one of my sisters was living with a Christian guy at the time, must have been very hard for my mother. She was still trying to come to terms with the death of our father.

Muhsin had already completed his studies by now with exemplary distinctions and was teaching at a local mosque. These years were very turbulent for my mother. She was shocked even further when Muhsin, the family hero and community role model, 'came out of the closet'. He announced to everyone that he was gay! His marriage was dissolved and he was fired from his post at the mosque. The impact that all of this had on our mother must have been more than any mother should have to bear. Understandably she took ill. This was, however, not the first time. The family she fought to keep together and on the right path, was falling apart. Her own family didn't exactly make things easier for her. They accused her of being too lenient with Muhsin. They pressurised her to sever all her ties with him and said things like: 'As a leader in our community you should lead by example.'

I could not blame Muhsin for coming out. He was not

responsible for all this happening because he was just being true to himself. He was also being honest and fair to his wife. I didn't linger on the revelation because I had my own issues to focus on at the time. I left him to 'sort out the mess he had made'. I felt that Muhsin was a big boy and he must take responsibility for his 'choices'.

The gay people I met, we called *moffies*. I must say that their exaggerated effeminacy was not something I was used to, or comfortable with. It made me very uncomfortable with, and prejudiced toward gays. My understanding of a *moffie* was a person that had problems relating to women because they felt inadequate as men, and therefore stuck to their own sort.

I also found out that there were young guys in the community that were hanging out with rich, white, homosexual men. They were providing sexual favours in return for money, expensive gifts and even drugs. These factors further fuelled my prejudice.

This was my negative perception of the gay community. I had no experience of any other gay people or the gay community to know any different than what I was seeing daily.

I was also hit on a few times by *moffies* and it really irked me. It was something awful. I grew to dislike them intensely and could not bear to be in their presence. From then on, I tried to avoid places where they usually gathered, but most hair salons at the time employed 'these kinds of people'. I once went to a salon to get a haircut and found myself confronted by a man who was touching my thighs and caressing my shoulders in ways that made my skin crawl. I then swore I would never visit salons again.

Now that I was confronted with a brother who was gay, this brought the past negative visions into my head. I could not believe that my very own brother could be like 'them'. It was a challenge that took me a while to digest. To help me along, I was fortunate to be approached by Parvez Hussein Sharma who directed a documentary film called *A Jihad for Love*. It was about the lives of queer Muslims. Muhsin featured as one of the selected characters to feature in the film. Parvez arranged a private viewing for my family and I, which was followed by a question and answer session. I was allowed to interact with him and Muhsin and it helped me to realise the dynamics of a gay person. I could thus understand their need for and their right to love. More profoundly I learnt the need for homophobic people, such as myself to accept them. Firstly, we need to accept queer people as human beings with inalienable rights. Secondly, we need to accept them as Muslim beings, with God given rights to express their love in a way that they feel comfortable. I could really relate to this documentary and the discussion. I now understood that my brother, who had never truly been accepted as a person by our family, was just looking for love. He needed to see that we cared about him and did not deny him the right to be his true self. It was through this new understanding that I became interested in the work that Muhsin was doing.

One evening, after this mind-blowing experience, I was relaxing at home with the radio on. It was the local Muslim radio station. I heard a discussion about homosexuality within Islam. I recognised my brother's voice coming out of the speaker. A sense of pride washed over me because of his commitment and free expression. I was surprised at his zest and valour in speaking about himself this publicly. He was also discussing, not only his own feelings, but also those of his fellow Muslim gay peers. Furthermore, he was engaging with the Muslim clergy and he was holding himself very positively amidst all these revelations.

There was a phone-in section later in the programme and people were allowed to ask questions, or give their comments. Most people that phoned in had negative comments and one guy actually threatened Muhsin on air. I became a little concerned for him because this guy was not interested in engaging with the issue; he had already made up his mind. He was convinced that his interpretation of the Quran was the only one and that there's no space for any other interpretation. What I couldn't understand was how our *ulema* could interpret the Quran in a way that was actually contrary to the true nature of Islam, which is about peace and love. Yet these people are the leaders in our community.

I have come to terms with my brother and I have learnt to accept people for who they are. I still, however, have so many questions for the people in our community that do not want to accept people who are not the same as them.

Is it our decision to judge whether queer people are right or wrong? Do people make choices about their sexuality or are they born with an attraction to the same sex? Do we as a community actually take the time to investigate these phenomena? Or do we just blindly condemn gay people because of our own lack of understanding and our self-serving interpretation of the scripture?

If it is that Allah in his infinite wisdom has created people this way (and there is scientific evidence to suggest that it is the case) what are we then really saying when we cast people out of the fold of Islam because of their sexual orientation? Are we denying what Allah creates? Are we saying that we are greater than Allah, in that we can choose to accept what we wish to accept from Allah? Are we then denying, with full acknowledgement, that Allah doesn't matter?

These are just a few questions that our choices may lead to. This is the road it will go down and this is where we'll end up. We need to decide.

14

Happiness

I sit on the sandy beach looking at the peaceful ocean. The sun's rays play on the water and reflect the things most close to the surface. The waves pound on the rocks and there is a slight wind in the air. It reminds me of the life I've lived, although mine was more turbulent. I sit on a rock and let my feet sway back and forth just below the surface, trusting those spaces I cannot see. I sit and wonder what is happening below the surface? Was it just me, or are there many others who have had to endure the same kind of life that I have.

Further along the beach is a family bathing on the beach. It seems as if they are apparently enjoying their time together. They look so happy, so naive, and at peace with each other. Is it a façade? Or are they really a happy family? Do happy families exist?

Playing nearby them is a little boy who is obviously their little son. Will he have to endure the same things as I have? Will he suffer the torment, the loss, the deceit and abandonment that I had to? Clearly there's something I need to get off my chest. I need a good ear to listen to my story. If you are a parent, please pay particular heed, this may be the story of your child. This may even be your story. You may be going through the same things that I have. In any case this story has elements that you will definitely be able to relate to it. So please as you read it, draw the lessons as you continue. Listen please...

The first recollection of my mother was that she left me in a shoebox in front of a neighbour's house. She was sixteen years old and I was only a few months old. She left me just like that. At the time she was married to my father, but that did not matter to her. She felt she couldn't raise me. So she disappeared and left me with my father, never to return again. My father remarried and I considered this new woman to be my mother, not my stepmother. This was the only maternal figure I have ever known. Our relationship wasn't very rosy and it soon became an abusive one. I believe that the reason for this was because she couldn't always get her way with my dad and then she would take it out on me. I was well-clothed, had the best of foods and had all the material possessions and luxuries that any heart could desire. But, my heart was not satisfied. I didn't receive the love that I needed.

This was my mother's second marriage and she had three children of her previous marriage. She treated us differently. The three stooges, as I thought of them at the time, were well treated. I was treated as 'step'.

The relationship was threatened even more with the arrival of my new stepbrother. It thus seemed as if there were three factions of siblings. This birth created a greater level of competition for attention. There were constant fights between the siblings. I was always treated as the scapegoat. On one occasion, I ended up with a fractured skull and my left hand was so badly injured that it is still not fully functional today.

Through all my ill-treatment I still regarded my stepmom as my mother because she instilled Islamic morals, values and ethics in my life. I was also staunch in my religious beliefs and strengthened myself with the verses *Luqman* and *Al-Ahqaf* (The Curved Sandhills) in the Quran that encouraged obedience to one's parents. I sometimes wondered about these references because they emphasise the obedience of mothers because children are born from the wombs of their mothers. So, I wondered whether this included stepmothers. I was convinced by religious leaders that I should reference my parents, regardless of the biological origins. I obeyed what I was taught. Let me not meander too much, but the role of parents is worth some consideration. The Quran states that 'We have enjoined on man (to be good) to his parents: in travail upon travail did his mother bear him, and in years twain was his weaning: (hear the command), 'Show gratitude to Me and to thy parents: to Me is (thy final) goal.'

I grew up with many struggles for acceptance. It was a battle to exist in the family and thus I never ever had the guts to tell them that I was gay. I was forced to go on *hajj* and to take *hafiz* classes. I thought pilgrimage wasn't allowed as it was improper to go to Mecca as a gay man. So, it was a very scary experience to go, but it was truly a memorable experience. It also provided me with an opportunity to see a different perspective on life. When I came back, I was considered a learned man and people would come to me for religious guidance and social support. I enjoyed the *hafiz* classes and I can still beautifully recite the Quran from memory. I enjoyed learning about the Quran as it also shed more light on my understanding of the religion.

My Islamic studies took first preference and I found it almost impossible to handle my schooling at the same time. My faith was strong that whenever I was under pressure and found it difficult to cope, I would make *salaah* and I would be able to focus again. It is the *salaah* that kept me sane. The reason that it kept me grounded was the fact that most people merely regard *salaah* as prayer, as per the common simple translation. To me, however, *salaah* in the true sense is much more. *Salaah* in Islam is a unique institution. It brings man closer to Allah by harmonising his mental attitude with physical posture. In *salaah*, a person submits himself completely to his creator.

When I matriculated, I enrolled at UNISA to study a course in tourism and it was funded by my dad. I was still very passionate about my religious studies and I wanted to become a leader in the field. Questions then arose about whether I could be gay and an imam. Yes, I went on Hajj and did extensive studies in the religion, but it just didn't feel right to become a community icon as a gay imam. In order to gain a better understanding of my sexuality, I studied the story of Sodom and Gomorrah in the Quran and found that there were things I couldn't understand, accept and apply to my life. I then tried dating a girl, but it did not work out.

'Hello – you are gay!' I told myself.

The voice of my past experiences rang out: 'This is just a phase! You will find a nice girl to get married to!'

Things were coming to the fore. I immersed myself in the Quran. I discovered a different interpretation of the story of Prophet Lut (may peace be upon Him) in Sodom and Gomorrah. This view stated that sexual practice during this era was about lewdness, incest and rape. It was not about relationships between same sex couples. My views were challenged. I discovered that the Quran itself does not condemn homosexuality, but rather that it was people's interpretations of it that created the condemnation of homosexuality.

I thought that the time had arrived for me to speak to my parents about my sexual orientation. However, I did not have the opportunity to do so. Before I developed the courage to speak to my parents, my mother interceded. I often wonder, even today still, if she could possibly have had a premonition that I wanted to discuss my sexuality. I guess all the discussions that I initiated made it evident that I was gay. I must confess that I was still undergoing great confusion about what choices to make. I still somehow at that time believed that homosexuality was wrong. I even spoke to my parents about a girl I liked, but there was still a blockage. My family always had difficulty in maintaining open communication about sexuality that we could never really engage with the topic.

Out of the blue, my mother gave my father an ultimatum which was that either I left, or she and her children would leave. She said that I was possessed with the devil. Imagine if I had to really bring up the topic of homosexuality! He chose them. I tried to clear things up with my mother, but she remained adamant.

I thus did not have the opportunity to 'come out' to my parents.

My dad cut off my tuition allowance. I realised that I was always excluded from my family, even when we went for Hajj. So I packed up and left. I was sad to leave my father and still maintained my respect for him; even kissing the ground he stood on before I left. I swopped my *salaah* tops for jeans when I left Durban for Johannesburg.

When I got to Johannesburg, I went to live with my blind aunt and immediately started with a new job. I met a Malay girl who I really liked, even though no one else liked her. We shared a strong bond and I spoilt her because I felt like I should. I also felt like I was being tested because of me being gay. We became very close and eventually I asked her to marry me. She agreed and a glamorous affair was planned. It was set to be a costly affair. I really went all out because I didn't want anyone to have anything bad to say about it.

I knew that it was all pointless. I couldn't run and hide from myself. I was who I was. I couldn't expect her to 'make me straight'. My gayness was gnawing at me. I tried to forget about it, hide it, contain it, but it just didn't work. It finally cracked me and I had to call off the wedding. It almost killed my fiancé, but I couldn't let her go through her life with a husband who wasn't really giving it his all. I couldn't let myself live a lie throughout my life. She broke all communication with me after that. I guess it was for the best.

My best friend Sharon stuck with me. She was the one that warned me that if I got married to a female, it would be a mistake. She explained that getting married and trying to forget about my gayness would only result in unhappiness. She always supported me and was always honest about everything. I've known her since childhood so generally we did everything together. To me she was like my guardian angel; we knew everything about each other. She helped me through this difficult episode in my life. She also helped me to come to terms with my sexuality and forming my identity. She gave me the strength to live my life regardless of what other people may say.

During the short time that I was living with my aunt, we developed an extremely close bond. I loved her dearly. She became dependant on me to be her eyes. When I revealed to her that I was gay, she didn't agree with it, but respected me for who I was.

After this episode, people started calling me a 'Luchman', which is a derogatory slang term for an Indian, cross-dressing transsexual. This infuriated me, but being rooted in my faith; I retaliated by ignoring them. I prayed for them and I prayed for myself, and I hoped that they would change because I believe in respect. I am also just a jovial, funny kind of person that can see the humour in many serious situations.

After the failed attempt at marriage, I changed my job and was now working at a bank. The thought of relationships became more complicated. I decided that I would merely continue with electronic dating on a chat site, Mig33. Many chats later, I soon connected with someone called Ederies. We merely stayed in contact via the chat site as I was hesitant to connect with anyone at this stage. Hence we did not exchange numbers or meet. I also had many chat buddies at this stage and was learning many new things.

I still had many girls approaching me, even though they could see I was not interested. There was one girl that was completely upset that I did not want to date her because she wanted so much to be with me. She threw a hissy fit, and stayed away from work for a week. I couldn't believe it. I decided to change jobs again as I was there for a shorter period than she was.

One day I was texting a friend on Mig33 and decided to rather call her instead. We were familiar with each other and shared a plutonic relationship. When I tried to call her, I went down one digit too far and called Ederies instead. We ended up in a heated conversation about the call. The more I tried to explain that I was attempting to connect with my other friend, the more he didn't want to understand. We decided to meet and eventually we started dating.

One day, when I am cleaning the house, my uncle walks in and asks me 'Are you gay?'

I told my sixteen-year-old sister that I was gay, but I swore her to secrecy. She told my uncle who had been monitoring me for a while. I could not deny it and I told him that I was. A shouting match soon followed where I let him know that I wasn't about to let him talk to me the way he wanted to, and that I was not going to change for anyone, least of all him.

After that episode, the news spread through my family like wildfire and I was soon bombarded by phone calls from the family enquiring about the unbelievable news. You would swear that someone was getting married, or having a baby. I was so upset with my family that I dressed myself in a skimpy top and a very tight pair of jeans, and paraded in front of everyone.

I then dated a different person, someone whom I liked very much. He eventually went as far as to introduce me to his mother and we hit it off immediately. I have no idea why we broke up. It wasn't something dramatic, otherwise I would remember, but I can't even think of one thing that either of us did wrong. So, maybe we just grew apart.

A few weeks went by before I received a call from the one person I thought would have called first: my dad. He asked me what everyone else was asking. I answered in the same way: 'Yes, I am.' My tone implied a heavy 'so what' attitude.

He then responded to this very calmly by saying that I should consider him and his family completely dead to me and that no one is supposed to live like 'that'. He said that I should fetch everything that was mine from his house. He also said that I should get it immediately because if I do not fetch it, he was going to throw it away himself.

I became the secret that no one spoke about; the ghost between the rafters. When I fetched my stuff, I told him that it saddened me that he felt this way and that I had to leave in this manner. I then told him exactly how I felt when he threw me out because of his wife and how he chose them over me. I reminded him of everything that I've ever done in that house and for that family: how I paid the bills, cleaned the house and generally how good a son I was. I told him of how he wasn't even there for me when I wanted to become independent. When I finally decided to get a car, he totally rejected me. I was almost begging for his love. Yes, I still love him.

Then, it finally hit me that I really am dead to him now. I told myself that he needs to accept me for who I am and that I can't hide myself to keep other people comfortable.

I felt completely lost from my family. I was alone.

I started seeing a guy called Emile and while we were together we found out he was dying of cancer. My world was torn apart. Everything that was bottled up inside of me came out: my mom's denial when I was growing up, my father abandoning me, my family exiling me and now this. It all came crashing down on me. So just before he died, because I couldn't stand being left alone again, I took my old school tie and hung myself from the cupboard railing. When that broke, I drank bleach and tried to kill myself again. Sharon caught me drinking the bleach and she then made sure I cleaned myself out and that I took anti-depressants.

'You need to be strong,' she said, 'just think of all those children out there who you are being a role model for. They are looking up to you because you stood up and said you're gay, and now you want to kill yourself? You can't do that to them.'

I nodded, vaguely aware of what she was telling me. I needed to check myself and stay on track. All I wanted was to be happy.

I sat thinking about this and realised that I had all I needed in this life to live comfortably, and I was. I was just basing too much of my existence on what other people thought of it and me. I had a place of my own, a car that I was paying off, and a respect that no one could remove.

In order to find out more about myself, I decided to find out who my biological mother was. I thought that this might help me to find peace within myself. I wasn't too happy with what I found. Apparently, after she left me and my dad, she had turned to prostitution because her family wouldn't accept her again. As a result, I had several siblings who remained unnamed, but I felt no need to find out who they were. I found myself wanting to help her, but I just couldn't because I didn't want her to know it was coming from me. I didn't want to have to go down a road that was never meant to be created.

I soon started asking myself whether I had done enough. Whether I could have done more for my family. Whether I should return and try to beg my father's forgiveness... but I decided no. I would then be taking back everything I now stood for.

I finally felt free and comfortable in whom I am now. Why should I feel bad or sad about what happened. It wasn't I who threw them away. It wasn't me who told my dad that he was dead to me. I have finally grown comfortable with the idea of me being an openly gay man, and I wasn't going back.

I told myself that all I had to do was wait and eventually my family would come around, and they did. They are not wholly happy about it, but they have learnt to accept me for who I am, and not what I am. But my dad still remains out of reach, his stubbornness shining through and through. But I cannot change that. Just as I must be who I am, he must be who he is. He must do what he feels is right.

I hope that as the water ebbs and flows from the shore, so too may you change and adapt to those around you, while remaining true to yourself. Only then can you truly be happy.

This is my life and only I can stand accountable for it before God, no one else!

15

Daddy's boy

As a child, I was always a daddy's boy and I would spend a lot of time with him. I would also help my mother in the home, more so than my other brothers did. It was wonderful to be at home. I was the baby in the family, so I was always spoilt. I got whatever I wanted, whenever I wanted it. My father was always my best friend and I hero-worshipped him. He would never put me down. I was a chubby child and it knocked my self-esteem. My dad was always the one to boost my spirits.

Due to my low confidence levels, I had very few friends at primary school. There was also nobody that I could consider a close friend. My schoolmates were also very mean and picked on me as if I was target practice. They would call me names based on my weight. I really wasn't too fond of school because of these incidents but eventually just put up with the names they called me over and over again. The result was a very introverted helpless little boy. My mom didn't help much as she discouraged me my relationships and was apprehensive about me bringing friends home. She also never allowed me to go out on weekends. Socialising was confined to spending time with my brothers and cousins.

I would spend many hours alone at home. This time was spent on searching through the house from room to room. I stumbled on my mom's shoes and decided to wear them. It was a fascinating new game for me. I also immediately became drawn to her clothing. She had always worked in the retail industry and therefore had a real sense of fashion and this appealed to me. This new game of wearing my mother's garments provided me with a sense of false pride. Whenever I was alone, I would feel great in prancing around like my mother and imitate her in the mirror. I also thought that I looked better in her clothing than I usually did. I continued this ritual all the way into my second year of high school.

Towards the senior grades of primary school I was a bit more at peace with myself. It was easier to communicate with the girls than with the boys. In fact, the boys never really spoke any sense and always made me feel very uncomfortable. At the time I couldn't understand the reason for the discomfort.

The first encounter I can recall that brought a dash of confidence into my system was with James. He was one of the bullies that always teased. I am not too sure if I can call him a friend, but with nothing more than acquaintances at that time, I guess he could qualify as friend. One morning he was standing at the school's front gate with a parcel in his hand.

'Who are you waiting for?' I asked him. He ignored me. I smiled to myself as I realised that he was shy and embarrassed. I realised that I knew the reason for him waiting there. Her name was Sarah Jacobs! She was one of the prettiest girls in school, and I had noticed him watching her on the playground.

'So what did you get her?' I asked when he didn't reply.

'It's none of your business!' he shouted at me, while attempting to kick me.

He turned back to the gate and concentrated on looking for Sarah. I mocked him as he so often mocked me. I enjoyed it immensely as other children gathered around and joined in the big tease that I had launched. They were reeling in laughter.

In a blink James was in front of Sarah and he gave her the package. She seemed to consider this for a moment and then kissed him on his cheek. He then took her hand and they walked into the school grounds together.

I said some mocking things to tease him. The crowd continued laughing behind me. I felt vindicated for all the years of rebuke and torment that I suffered.

In a moment the answer was clear. The solution to all my problems was to find a good looking and popular 'girlfriend' and everyone would stop making fun of me. *The key to a successful future lie in finding the perfect girl!* I found a girl that everyone thought was attractive. I bought her things like chocolates, sweets and little presents. It did the trick to provide me with some confidence. All went well until the day I found her kissing another boy on the field. I realised that I could not provide her with the things that were important to her and let the relationship go. I went on to the next girl that was available. This was about one thing and one thing only. It was about building my affirmation. I wasn't going to allow myself to get hurt again. I made every effort to prove to myself and to the other children that I was just as good as them. This attitude and behaviour continued all the way to high school, and I couldn't stop myself. For a short while I became like them, mean and vicious. It was my protection. Eventually it was no longer an act; it became a part of my character. Selecting a girlfriend became a thing to impress others, rather than to find a compatible companion.

I came home from school one day and there was a strange silence in the house. I was told that my father was ill. It left me feeling stressed and lost. My greatest friend was in hospital. There was no one to turn to and to confide in. I was left to deal with the world on my own. Mother wouldn't tell us what was wrong with him, but I knew it was serious. She was crying profusely and would often disappear and lock herself in her bathroom or bedroom. I would try to make her smile or laugh, but nothing worked.

He was there for a while and I could only visit him over the weekend. I was sad because my support was no longer available. It was even worse when mom all of a sudden told us that we couldn't go with her any more. She was the only one that could visit him. I could see that this was aging her, so I'd do what I could around the house to make life a little easier for her.

I really missed my dad as I was simultaneously going through a bad patch. I had just started high school. I was confronted with dealing with my sexual identity and discovering the controversies of adolescence. I was searching for new horizons and trying to conquer the world. These challenges I had to face alone. I realised that my uncertainty with boys was because I was attracted to them. I didn't really notice it in primary school, but now I just couldn't control myself. Everywhere I went, there were guys and I couldn't help finding them attractive. I was also more popular as I was on the school soccer team. I was really feeling the crunch!

A month after this drawn out period, my mother came home and she wasn't crying anymore. It looked as if the fountain of tears had just run dry. Traces of tears were on her cheeks, but they were not wet. I wondered what was going on. It was unusual. My brothers were out while I was doing the dishes. It was only the two of us.

'What's wrong, Mom?' I asked her.

She was really quiet for a long while and then she spoke only two words: 'He's dead.'

'Who…' I started asking, but then I realised who she was talking about. I became light-headed. My head was filled with questions, but although I tried, I couldn't voice most of them.

'I thought he wasn't that sick?' I asked.

'He wasn't, but his condition changed suddenly and now…' she drifted back into her stupor. It took me a moment to collect myself and then I hugged my mother. We sat in a locked embrace until my brothers walked in.

'Dad died today,' I explained as they took their seats around my mother.

The *janaazah* was the following day. Although he was ill, it was extremely difficult to recover from the trauma. It was especially hard on me. I dealt with it by taking up smoking. It helped soothe the pain. I was more at a loss because I did not have my dad to talk to about my sexuality, which was still foremost in my mind. Smoking also helped to disguise the guilt about not telling my mother about my sexuality. It consumed my whole being.

I also had very strong religious beliefs and it caused greater confusion in dealing with my identity. It was my understanding that Islam condemned homosexuality. But I started thinking about how God wanted me to be happy, and he wouldn't make me this way if he didn't want me to be this way. I accepted this realisation, and was never affected by questions about my sexuality and my religion. I became more concerned about my family and what they would think. I feared their responses to this news. I didn't want them to find out and so I went clubbing to minimise the time that I spent at home. Clubbing was taboo in my family, so I lied about it. I would say that I'm going to a friend's house, but then would go to the club instead. At the clubs I soon realised that drinking made my issues more bearable. So now I was smoking, clubbing and drinking. It soon spiralled out of control.

A few years later, on a Saturday afternoon, my mother insisted that we spend the day with our family. We went over and I dealt with their drab conversation for most of the day, but I went outside as evening set in. My cousin was sitting with a friend in the neighbour's backyard. He tried to hide from me. This made me curious, so I went closer. Then I noticed that they were smoking *tik*.

'Moeneeb, where'd you get that?' I asked him, interested.

'We got it from a merchant that lives down the road,' he laughed, making his friend laugh too.

'Can I join you?' I asked without really thinking. I guess it was because they were laughing and seemingly so happy and I thought that it might be able to take me completely away from my issues.

'Ja,' he said, and then returned to the globe before him. I joined but I just didn't feel anything. It made me frustrated as I was not feeling as happy as I thought I would. We started walking back to the house and I scolded most of the time.

'This is crap!' I ranted, 'I don't feel anything, and you mustn't come to my house again with this, because it does nothing.'

I had been attending a technical college for the past two years, but I was now forced to drop out as I didn't have any more funding to continue, so I started working at Topics. I noticed that people avoided me in the mall and I decided that I needed to do something about my weight. I went on a healthy eating spree and I joined a gym. Two to three months down the line, I was slender. People would mock me because I was too thin in my clothing. I changed my wardrobe and wore tight-fitting clothing that suited me. I felt much better about myself. This, however, led to another situation. I was now always very well dressed and people started questioning me about the one question that I didn't want to answer or accept.

'Are you gay?' they asked me. They didn't use those exact words, but that's what it came down to.

'Are you mad?!' I'd ask angrily. 'Me? Do I look gay?'

'Well, you dress so well, and you look so good, what are we supposed to think?'

No matter what their justifications were, I just felt that I didn't want to tell them. I was also in denial.

These questions increased in number as the time went on and I soon found myself craving something. It took me a while to realise what it was, and it turned out to be *tik*.

I went out looking for it, and soon found a dealer close to my place. I found that I enjoyed it much more the second time. I felt numbed to everyone's questions and I went zooming through life on a constant high. I continued to use it and I found that I became a lot more comfortable with guys when I was all smoked up. I then started using with guys that were comfortable with my sexuality.

I particularly liked one of my new friends, Shaheen. We became what one may call tik-buddies and I brought him home and we would sit in my room and get high. One evening as we were high, we were lying on my bed and he started stroking his fingers across my leg. I was unaware at first because my sensations were numb from the chemicals. I only became aware of what he was doing when he touched my hand. He put his fingers in mine and the next thing I knew we were kissing. This continued for the next few times that we were using and then things just spiralled out of control.

My mother found out about my addiction when a group of users came to my house looking for me. I was sent to rehab the next day, and although I was dedicated to recovery, I left rehab close to completion. I went back into my routine of drugging with Shaheen until I decided that I needed to make a clean sweep and stop using *tik*. I enrolled myself into a new programme and then remained in there until I was 'clean'.

When I left I had to break ties with Shaheen as he was still addicted. I felt I loved him and so I decided to have one more meeting with him. We shared that evening together and everything felt so right that I expected him to call me the following day, or in the week, but no such call came. It was difficult to accept. It took me three years to finally get over him.

After being 'clean', it was once again difficult to talk to guys. I started using man-to-man dating lines because they were anonymous. I found it easy to talk to guys as I could be very open with them because they didn't know me. I could talk to them face-to-face and not feel ashamed because they wouldn't recognise me afterwards.

I met a guy named Shabier online. He was younger than me but the way he chatted was interesting and we just clicked instantly. I could chat with him for hours. I would also felt bad if I didn't reply quickly enough or not at all. Eventually we decided to meet. We started spending a lot of our time together and I introduced him to my family. He visited regularly. My brothers were always sceptical of the relationship, but I didn't let it bother me as I was enjoying myself with Shabier. They were finally realising that I am not merely going through another crazy phase. They also had conflicting information as

I still dated girls for affirmation reasons, but they didn't know this.

On the weekend, we went to a braai at Shireen's house. She was a very good friend of mine. My friends were acquainted with Shabier as he accompanied me everywhere. We were inseparable. As I was standing alone by the fire, Shireen approached me.

'So what's the story?' she asked me.

'With what?' I asked her as I fanned the smoke away from my face.

'You and Shabier,' she said. 'You take him his food, you can't sit apart, you need to sing together when we karaoke and I am surprised that you're now standing alone at the fire. You're never apart...'

'He's gone to the loo,' I swiftly commented, trying to steer the conversation in a different direction.

'Are you gay?' she cut in, forcing out the words. I felt my heart race, but I couldn't let this affect me. I tried to control my response, but I don't think I succeeded.

'I've told you that I'm not!' I spoke through gritted teeth.

'Fine,' she replied, 'but when you're ready to talk, then I will be available.' She stalked off back to the house as Shabier headed toward me.

'What was that about?' he asked, as he leaned over the fire-place to heat his hands.

'She wanted to know if I'm gay,' I told him. I felt so frustrated that I wanted to hug him and get it out of my system, but I clearly couldn't.

'Maybe you *should* tell her,' he said, and I looked at him incredulously. 'She is your best friend, and she probably knows already.'

I thought about this and he had a point. We've always shared everything, good and bad. We knew each other's flaws and shortcomings. She even helped me through my drug addiction. So, I decided that I should tell her.

I asked Shabier to take care of the braai, while I went inside. I took her hand and led her to her room. I closed the door and sat her down. I told her everything.

'I'm bisexual...' I told her. All she did was nod knowingly, and then I told her about every guy I'd been with including Shaheen and Shabier.

'Thanks for telling me but I still feel you're lying to me, and yourself... but that's okay. Once you're ready to come out completely, I'll be there for you,' she said as we hugged. I hastened back to join Shabier at the braai and I smiled at him as he handed me the tongs.

On my way home, I realised how comfortable I was with Shabier and how good he made me feel. For the first time I didn't have the voice in my head telling me this was wrong. I was totally happy.

Our relationship continued wonderfully until he started using drugs, abusing me and using me to get him to parties. The breakup was traumatic. This was the worst moment in my life, other than my father's death. I had a relapse because I needed to mask my fears again. I grew to pity myself.

Soon I realised that I needed help. I was sinking into the same pit as before. I explained the situation to my manager and told her I needed to go for treatment. She was very accommodating and helped me on my way to recovery.

During the first few sessions I realised that I needed to get away from my lies and I needed to tell my family the truth. I told them I was bisexual.

My mother was stunned at first but then hugged me. I think her acceptance was motivated by the fact that my dad was gone, and she didn't want to lose another part of her family. My one brother came to me and said he'd known all along, and that he was just waiting for me to 'come out' on my own. My eldest brother couldn't handle the news. He merely got into his car and drove off. I could understand this as he was part of the Islamic society and he was a member in the nearby mosque.

This was against Islamic laws, so he couldn't accept it. The next time I saw him, he just refused to be seen with me. All he said was that I should come see him when I'm over this guy thing and when I'm ready to settle down with a woman.

I continued with the programme and found myself confronting my sexuality. I realised and accepted the fact that I didn't feel for girls the same as what I felt for guys. I accepted that I was gay and not bisexual. That same day I went to my mother and told her the absolute truth. All she did was hold me and cry. I think it still bothers her but she tries to hide it as much as possible.

It may be an over-used cliché, but I sincerely believe that the truth can set one free.

16

New beginnings

I look out the window at the crimson sun reflecting off the rooftops in the distance. A new dawn has risen and I feel energised as I open my eyes to greet the world. I am so fortunate to be living in an apartment in an affluent area with wide windows that need not be curtained. Then I slowly cuddle up next to my boyfriend who slowly turns around and smiles. He looks extremely satisfied as he lies snuggled up beneath the sheets with only his head and arms showing. I am so proud to be with him. He is a few years younger than I am but that doesn't have any bearing on how I feel about him. We love each other unconditionally but it took us many years to get to this point. Our love is apparent and reflects in the very essence of our being. There is no need for words in this relationship. I can easily tell he loves me from the way he looks at me. Our love is displayed on the bedroom door: 'SALIE LUVS YAZEED', printed in bright bold letters and stuck on a bright pink heart.

My life has never been this happy before. It wasn't exactly sad or traumatised like many other queer folk, but it had its challenges like any other person. In a way I often think that I had it fairly easy. I will let you decide what you feel about my story as I share it with you. I hope that it will speak to you in some way…

I was about four years old when I had my first homosexual experience. 'Impossible' you think? Well, I was molested by my father, so it was not by choice. My mother had been gone for a while to look after my granny who lived a few hours' distance away from us. My father had to take care of me. I was happy to spend time with my father because he always had fun things lined up to keep me entertained. This time was different. He started playing with me in a manner that I did not understand. I don't remember all the details, but I do remember the fact that he played with me sexually, or so I was reminded. According to my mom, I told my teacher all about it the next day when I went to crèche.

Naturally, she was concerned, and contacted my mother about it. My mother was at the school in thirty minutes flat. I then repeated to her what I told the teacher and the principal. The principal then called the police. They came an hour later and my mother cried for some reason that I couldn't understand. I rubbed my hand up and down her back to comfort her, and I smiled at her and said 'It's okay, mommy.'

She cried louder and held me tight. I now know why she cried that day and why she was so upset. A man, whom she trusted and loved, sexually abused her child, and her child still thought that it was okay. She probably wasn't sure what was worse: her child's ignorance or her husband's injustices…

That was the last time I ever saw my father. I had always blamed my mother without realising the impact of the situation.

The years went by and a few days before my twelfth birthday, she asked me what I wanted as a present. She said I could have anything I wanted and I knew exactly what I wanted this year. I told her I wanted to know the truth about why my father left us. By then, I had completely forgotten about what had happened when I was four. I saw regret in her eyes. I could tell she wanted to retract her offer, but she knew I would insist on an answer. I stared deep into her eyes, waiting for an answer. She was never a good liar and I could tell if she was lying. She became uncomfortable and mumbled that she could not tell me the reason. I burst out of the room in a rage. 'You are a rotten liar,' I shouted, 'I HATE YOU!!!'

Slowly she followed me to the room. She was in tears. She took a deep breath and finally came out with the truth:

'Something happened when you were about four.' She said this as her throat tightened. 'I don't think you'll remember it, but your father did...' She took a moment to collect herself. 'He did something bad to you,' she said.

'Something like what, mom?' I asked insistently. 'The truth, Mom...'

She seemed to need a moment so I waited patiently and then she went on. 'He sexually molested you, Salie,' her voice rose as she said it. I watched her face contort from sorrowful to pure hurt. Her eyes filled with tears and I understood why my mother didn't speak about him or any part of my childhood.

I hugged her and I felt the pain run through her as she relived the encounter of that day. I felt horrible about bringing up the story. She hugged me again and we sat glued to each other for a while, until I felt her loosen her grip. She said that she was happy that it was all out in the open. She said I should go do my homework and she went off to carry on with whatever it was that she was doing.

I did well in school. It was my way of making my mother happy. She was proud of her son but she was troubled by the fact that I wasn't like the kids my age. I was about thirteen, when she asked me why I wasn't 'seeing anyone'. Thereafter she constantly asked me if I had a 'girlfriend'. My answer, like a stuck record, was always that I was not interested in anybody in that way because I was still in primary school and my friends were the people I preferred to spend my time with. It was true. I had to focus my attention on my school work and making my mother proud. There would be plenty of time to think about 'seeing someone' later.

Then came high school and I dreaded it at first. I'd have to make new friends because I attended a school outside our immediate neighbourhood. But it wasn't as hard as I had initially thought. I quickly adapted to my new environment and made friends just as fast. But things turned sour when my voice started breaking halfway through the year. People made fun of the high pitched sounds that emerged from my mouth. I tried hard not to let it bother me, but it upset my friends. *Don't get angry* I used to tell myself *they want a reaction, don't give them that satisfaction.*

There is this one day that I remember very clearly. My teacher was absent and I sat on the field with a couple of friends doing homework for the next period. Another class joined us there; they played soccer to pass the time. Nasser, one of my friends, decided to join them. He quickly changed into a pair of red shorts and a white shirt and made his way onto the field. As I turned to continue with my work there was a boy sitting next to us. He said something as he made himself comfortable, but I couldn't make out what it was.

'Excuse me?' I said. But he just shook his head as he stared out at the field, lost in thought. A little while later my friends made their way to the tuck shop, but I stayed behind because I wanted to finish my work. Suddenly, the boy moved closer. I was alarmed by what he said next: 'The boy in the red shorts looks yummy.' I looked at him, quite taken aback by his statement. He barely acknowledged that I was looking at him. *What?* I thought to myself, as I turned my attention to the field. Was he talking about Nasser? 'What did you say?' I asked, laughing at this absurd predicament. I mean, did he really just call another boy 'yummy'? Casually, he turned to me and said, 'Just look at him.' And for the first time I did. I really looked at Nasser! I noticed his muscles tighten and relax as he ran to kick the ball. Everything slowed down and faded into the background. Nasser was my focus of attention. I suddenly saw him in a different light. I was overcome by this strange hot feeling under my collar. *What's going on here?* I thought to myself. I hesitantly turned to the boy to further the conversation but he was gone. All that remained were his shoe tracks in the sand. When the bell rang, I grabbed my books and headed for the next class. I couldn't let my friends see me like this.

But as luck would have it they caught up with me just as I

walked into the room and sat around me. I felt claustrophobic and faint. But the problem wasn't with them; it was with what was going through my head. My thoughts focussed on the boys in my class. I saw them through new eyes. I didn't see them as boring or cool, funny or not, but rather as who was attractive and who was not. I became horrified and lost all emotional control. My friends were worried because I was all flustered. My red face showed symptoms of one who was sick. They rushed me to the sick bay. This is where I spent the rest of the school day. The time alone left me to my thoughts. I was stressing about what was happening to me. I rolled from one end of the bed to the other. My friends came to check up on me every now and again. During the last period, the boy that opened this new world came strolling in and sat down next to the bed.

I jumped up and moved away from him.

'What are you doing here?' I shouted at him. 'Who are you anyway?'

'I've been at this school for two years already,' he said. 'I am Nazeem Davids. I am gay, and I think you are too.'

I looked at him incredulously, and tried to figure this out.

'How can I be gay without knowing it?' I asked.

'Oh, you knew all along. Trust me, you knew, you just weren't aware of it,' he replied. 'Think about everything that happened today. You can blame it on me, but deep down inside of you, you know!' He laughed softly.

I was very uncomfortable with his smugness, but I couldn't argue with him. Just as I wanted to engage further he disappeared out the door. I felt that I couldn't deal with it at that time. It was my first year in high school and already there were so many changes taking place. Now I get confronted with this!

'Allah, what are you trying to tell me?' I continuously asked myself as I walked home. I was emotionally exhausted by all the new information playing around in my head. All my teachings said that a boy should not be with another boy. A boy should be with a girl. Yes, I needed to be with a girl. This was not acceptable in my community. So, I did not know how to deal with it.

When my mom came home, I asked her what the Quran said about gay people and she launched into an explanation of how wrong it was and how people like that were going to burn in *jahannam* and there's no way around that. Then she wanted to know the reason for my enquiry.

'One of the boys at school is gay and I wanted to know if it's okay to be...' I said.

She then went on a rampage of how I shouldn't be friends with him. She said that I should stay away from him because befriending him would mean that I was going to become gay as well and go to *jahannam* with him. At least the people would all talk about me in a bad way. The topic was interrupted with the entrance of Zaid, my mother's boyfriend. I guess I should be glad as it diffused the conversation.

Zaid was kind of cool, I guess. He treated my mom with respect and it was clear that he loved her. At this point it wasn't clear whether she loved him though. He would spend the entire weekend with us, but sleep in the guest bedroom. I didn't mind because he always made good conversation. We could talk about various things and when Sunday came around I felt sad to see him go.

I made up my mind. I wasn't going to say anything about being gay again. There was no way in hell (excuse the pun) that I was going to risk it because I feared that everyone would turn on me. I left all the questions and went on with my life as usual. It was not that bothersome because I was not really attracted to anyone. As time went by, however, I realised that my attraction towards other guys grew stronger.

After I completed my high school education, I decided I was going to experiment with this hidden feeling that lay deep within me. I found out about a cruising spot in the Cape Town Gardens. Here men would meet and become better acquainted. I thought that this was far from home and no one would know me. I felt fairly 'safe' and went on my journey to town. As I walked around, I saw men kissing and leaving together. I could not imagine what they did when they departed. I felt my body tingle at the thought as a picture darted through my mind. I blushed as I cleared my mind. I sat down quickly to hide my embarrassment. I thought of how I was going to deal with the situation, should it arise. I felt cheap and dirty in what I was doing, but I had no other option, my community was totally against homosexuality. Why couldn't I be myself at home? Surely the one place where I'm supposed to be safe and free is my home. I love my family but I could not engage with them. They only love me conditionally. Should they find out about me, they would not accept me – this I knew!

While I was sifting through my thoughts, a guy came to sit next to me. I became self-conscious and tried not to make a fool of myself. The guy was attractive, and a bit older than me. He smelt good. I laughed to myself and then tried to watch what he did and follow his lead.

He struck up a conversation with me about meaningless things and I found myself laughing at all his jokes. He was smart, funny and attractive too. He surprised me when he leaned over and kissed me. I didn't even see it coming and we were in broad daylight where everyone could see us, but I enjoyed it so I kept going. After all, my face was covered by his face, so no one could see me. But just as I let go of my fear, I heard someone call my name. I froze in shock as the voice registered. I looked up to find my mom's boyfriend standing there. He looked at me in disbelief. I wanted to burst of embarrassment. I thought that he was going to tell everybody and that my life was ruined. Instantly, horrid flashes went through my mind! I felt more dirty, ashamed and disgusted with myself. He indicated that I should come with him. I greeted the stranger and meekly trotted next to him with my head lowered to the ground.

'What's wrong? Why are you so silent?' he asked as I turned my face away. 'Since when have you known?' he continued after a drawn out pause. I couldn't answer.

'Speak to me,' he said, and then he realised what it was about. 'I won't tell anyone else. You can confide in me. 'You need to talk to someone and it might as well be me.'

I looked at him and he indicated that we should sit on one of the benches. I told him everything. He listened attentively and nodded occasionally. He didn't speak until I was finished, but only after a short silence, to allow for the story to be fully digested.

'My son, Irifaan, also came out four months ago and it's not easy.'

I looked up at him and saw that there were tears in his eyes. He had been dealing with his own issues that I didn't even know about.

'Does my mom know?' I asked.

'She knows that I have a son but not that he is gay. I don't know how she'll react,' he said with difficulty.

From that day onward he became my best friend. We shared all our stories with each other. Eventually I had an ear that would listen to my gay tales. I was so glad that he found me in the nick of time, before I made a fool of myself in the Gardens. We spoke at length and he became the father that I did not have. I enjoyed his company and looked forward to seeing him over the weekend.

On one of those weekends he offered to take me to a movie. We collected his son from his ex-wife and continued to the cinema. Irifaan was like a younger version of his dad. He was three years younger than me, but we clicked immediately. I felt honoured that I was the first one in the family to be introduced to his son. Thereafter, we spent a lot of time together. I was enjoying the relationship that was growing between us. I had acquired two close friends in a very short space of time. They were like a support system for me. I even started to go on outings with Irifaan without Zaid's presence.

One night, Zaid told me of his plans to propose to my mother. I told him that I would be ecstatic. He was, however, concerned about telling my mother about Irifaan. As we spoke, I suggested that he bring Irifaan to meet my mom. He agreed and the next weekend he brought Irifaan with him. My mother got along very well with him. The first day was spent chatting like a family. I felt so happy. We spent the entire weekend together, doing things together like a family.

On the Sunday morning, I woke with an uneasy feeling. My stomach was tied in knots. I had a premonition of what the day would hold. I feared my mother's reaction. This unsettled me.

Late that afternoon he asked her, 'Will you marry me?'

She stood there shocked, but after the shock wore off, she agreed.

As we sat in the lounge, Zaid said, 'There's only one thing I still need to tell you.'

'There's more?' she said excitedly.

'Well, yes,' he said. Then he looked at Irifaan sitting next to me. 'My son is gay,' he said, and my mother's face instantly became very stern. There was tension lurking in the air as we waited for her reaction.

'And you accept it?' she questioned. 'Does he practice it?'

'You make it sound like a cult!' Zaid said loudly, 'as if it's witchcraft!'

'You know what I mean…' she said. 'Does he or doesn't he?'

'He kisses other boys, yes,' he said, a bit abruptly.

'Get out,' she said.

'You just agreed to marry me,' he said, his eyes opening wide.

'Well, that was before I knew your son was a *mof*–' Zaid stopped her, and turned to his son.

'Go to the car, *kanalah*, Irifaan,' he instructed his son.

Before they could leave I was in tears. As Irifaan got to the door I shouted: 'Wait!'

Zaid came towards me and said: 'Not now Salie! Now is not the time!' He could sense what was going to happen. He stood beside me as I turned to my mother. He held my shoulder as I said, 'I am gay too, mom.' I said it a bit softly, but calm and direct.

She looked at me and seethed.

'This is your father's fault! That dirty, filthy son of a bitch! It's all he's fault!' She hissed, went to her room as she slammed the door. This was the first time that I ever saw my mother in this raged condition. Immediately she bounced right back and screamed, 'If he never did that to you, then you wouldn't be like this!' She was hysterical.

'Mom, do you think that Allah would let a man turn me into something that Allah doesn't want on this planet?' I said, crying. 'Allah loves me, and would never let me go through all this for no reason!'

'Get out,' she said, 'I don't want someone like you in my house. Get your stuff and get out. You can come back when you have changed.'

'I can't change what Allah made, *umi*,' I said softly.

'You can come live with me,' Zaid said. 'My house has two extra bedrooms, so there's enough space for you.'

I then went into my room and gathered my stuff.

As I headed towards the front door, I wanted to hug my mother, but she wouldn't let me. I left the house crying.

Zaid and Irifaan were waiting for me in the car.

That was the longest night of my life. I cried. I screamed. I felt so much pain. I wasn't sure I would survive it. I was so unsure about my future and what was to become of me.

As the next day dawned, I woke up to a new beginning. It was the start of a new chapter. A weight had been lifted off my shoulders and I was happy. I had a family that accepted me for who I am. Irifaan was now like a brother and Zaid was my father. I wondered if I'd ever see my mother again but knew that either way, I'd be okay. But life didn't become perfect overnight. It took years of struggle to get over it.

Irifaan introduced me to Yazeed a few years later and I'm still with him. This is the love of my life and we have moved on since then. Yes, I am now in a beautiful place called home, my third home ever.

I look at my bedroom door saying: 'SALIE LUVS YAZEED' and I feel content. Yazeed opens his eyes as he turns to look at me. I kiss him, so he knows that I love him. We cuddle, and as I cuddle in his arms, I pray: '*Shukran* Allah for everything that you have given to me! I'll never forget how far I've come. My life wasn't perfect and there are so many things that I have gone through. Yes Allah, in the end You guide us to where we can find the people that we're supposed to be with. You provide families! With your blessing I have eventually found absolute and unconditional love. Amen!'

17

The dreaded flight

The passengers are boarding the plane as I make my way to the check-in counter. I release a deep breath and wonder if I'll still feel this strong when I land on the other side. The attendant returns my boarding pass and I continue down the tunnel toward the aeroplane. My heart races a bit as I reflect on the life experiences that have brought me to this. I think of everything that happened and I acknowledge that this is a positive start to a new chapter in my life. I take my seat in the plane and I immediately buckle my safety belt. I am still a bit nervous of flying so I pray that this flight will pass quickly. People are still boarding and finding their seats as I close my eyes in order to centre myself and clear my head. I try to forget the reason for my flight to Port Elizabeth. This is impossible because it constantly flashes through my mind. I become irritated by these thoughts ricocheting in my mind.

The captain announces that we are about to take off and that everyone should sit back and fasten their seat belts. I concentrate on my breathing in order to prepare for the rapid change in pressure caused by the take-off. I relax completely as we take off, but I am jolted back to reality by the pressing need of my bladder. As soon as we reach our cruising altitude I undo my seatbelt and swiftly move to the toilet where I have to wait for someone to finish. The in-flight movie starts as I return to my seat. *What's the point?* I think to myself as I look at the screen, *the flight is only an hour long*. I close my eyes, in the hope of sleeping but there is a nagging feeling that keeps me awake. The reason for my trip challenges my thoughts. I need to speak to my father.

'One of the best ways to get rid of an issue is to retell your story. In so doing you can get it out of your head!' my counsellor's words ring in my ears.

Well here goes!

I was born into a happy, respectful home, close to the beach in PE. My mother loved us all dearly. My father encouraged collective values and promoted joint family outings. I remember our modest house looking so lonely when we marched off to the beach every Saturday morning. We looked like a troop of soldiers marching on the sand. I loved these family outings to the beach.

I was a bright kid, smarter than my peers and thus went to school a year earlier than the usual age. I was very inquisitive and sought answers to anything that I did not understand. My parents and sisters were very patient and would always respond to my often demanding requests. I loved them dearly. We were close knit and were always there to support one another.

Things changed in my fifth year of primary school. My mother was diagnosed with cancer and it changed our lives. My father ensured the best doctors and treatment for her, but the medical fund and other additional emergency funds soon ran dry. My mother decided to stop her treatment and stayed at home. She also said that she wanted to die at home with her family around her. *What had we ever done to warrant this from God?* I wondered. My father, being a God-conscious person at the time, said after the funeral, 'Jasmine, certain things need to happen to help us to get to where God wants us. Sometimes, it's to help us grow emotionally, mentally or physically.'

After my mother's death, my father lost his faith and went into a deep state of depression. When I reached high school, my sister and I were left with the responsibility of running the house and taking care of my dad. We also found part-time jobs to keep ourselves afloat financially. He eventually came out of his depression, found a secure job and fell back into his optimistic old routine.

But no sooner had he recovered, than he regressed. Every evening after work, he'd stop in at the local shebeen and have several drinks before coming home. Soon he started to stock alcohol at home and whenever we saw him, he was in a drunken stupor. It broke us to see our father in this state. It was unbecoming of him. I just couldn't stand by and lose him to alcohol because he was unreachable behind that wall of liquor. There were days when my sister would find me curled up crying because my father was in such a state. She would comfort me as best she could, but I still missed my parents.

I started dating to take my mind off the issues at home. Even though I didn't feel any connection with the various boys I dated, just being with them helped me to shut out the sad memories of my mother. Boys became my vice and my crutch, my own personal drug to help me cope and forget my sorrows. During my senior years at high school, I met Devon. He was head over heels in love with me. He wanted to be with me all the time and I didn't mind him being around because it took my mind off the many losses in my life. When I completed schooling we decided to express our physical attraction. Our first encounter created the fantasy that I was truly needed and that I eventually belonged to someone. It numbed the hurt of an empty house that was no longer a home. Sex became my new release and Devon was thrilled by it, but the relationship was empty. I felt trapped with him, but he was the only person that I really had, other than my sister.

Things at home were getting out of control. I needed to change my behaviour and advocate for change in our home. I suggested that we go for spiritual counselling. During the session, my father was at his lowest and he cried while he opened up to us. This broke me emotionally and I burst out crying. We sat there for a long time talking and crying. Dad said that he was ready to start afresh. The next day, however, he put us out. My sister had a permanent position at a local company close to home, so she had to live with family. I, on the other hand had to go to my aunt and uncle in Cape Town. At first I didn't want to leave, but I also didn't want things to be more difficult for him. So I packed up some things, explained the situation to Devon and left. He was devastated but said that he would wait for me.

I left the following week and I celebrated my twenty-first birthday in Cape Town with my aunt and uncle. It was a lonely celebration. I was home-sick and called my sister. She told me that she was back at home and was looking after Dad. I spent the rest of the night of my birthday in bed, crying like a baby. I wanted to be home with my family and this brought on another emotional outburst. I had a secure job with a small company in town, so I could not go to PE.

I once more played the dating game to take my mind off my loneliness and quickly made friends. I dated one guy after the next, very much similar to my high school days. I could not find anyone to satisfy my emotional needs. The years flew by and I was still filled with emptiness.

I stopped dating for a while and decided to just 'hang out' with friends. A colleague invited me to a party at her house in Sea Point. It was a lot more promising than a night at home. The place was completely packed. I went with my friend to the kitchen and she spoke to someone she apparently knew. I greeted her and she introduced herself as Shahiedah. I looked around the house and I noticed that something was different. It felt obvious but I couldn't really figure it out until a girl touched my leg rather weirdly. *There were no guys at this party!*

I was taken aback by this shocking discovery and tracked down my friend for further enquiries. On the way, I noticed two girls kissing one another. I felt slightly aroused by this and started imagining myself kissing one of the girls. Embarrassed, I shook my head, and continued my search. *What was I thinking?* When I reached my friend, she leant over and kissed the girl next to her passionately. I stopped, turned and started making my way to the door. I moved through the crowd, dazed by what I had seen. I sat there thinking what all this meant.

The penny dropped: my friend was a lesbian!

Everything that my religion taught me came rushing back to me. The cities of Sodom and Gomorrah were flashing through my mind. I saw the fire and brimstones falling down on this Sea Point house. I wrestled with the idea that all this was wrong, and yet I still wanted to be a part of it. I kept looking back at these girls, either kissing or just holding each other. As I stared, I realised that there didn't seem to be much difference between what they did, and what opposite sex couples did. They both kissed similarly, they both touched similarly and they both held each other in much the same way, so why would scripture say it is wrong?

I stayed sitting outside for a while, thinking about everything that happened and what it meant to me as a person, trying not to dismiss the teachings that were instilled in me. *It's not that different, how can it possibly be wrong?* I kept asking myself. I contemplated it over and over, until my friend finally came outside to look for me. She sat next to me and brushed my hair out of my face. I jumped back a little, not realising it was her.

'I'm sorry I didn't tell you,' she sighed, 'I was just afraid you would decide not to come.'

'You're right,' I said. 'I probably wouldn't have come,' I smiled at her knowingly, and sighed loudly.

'So what do you want to do now?' she asked me.

'I think I'm going to stay here, and think about a few things,' I replied. 'Go in and enjoy the party.'

'At least come inside,' she said, 'it's freezing out here.' She lifted me by the elbow and I joined her in the kitchen. From there I could see everything and so it was the perfect place to discover more about this new lifestyle.

I spent the entire night watching females kiss, caress and touch each other. It seemed very refreshing from what I did as part of a 'normal couple'. I was baffled and couldn't understand what it was that made these relationships taboo. It looked so natural and beautiful.

As I struggled to compose my thoughts, a girl came to sit next to me.

'Hey,' she said, as she sipped her drink.

'Hey,' I replied, and then returned to my observations.

'I'm Shire,' she introduced herself, and extended her hand towards me.

'I'm Jasmine,' I replied hesitantly, cautiously taking her hand. We shook hands and then I immediately withdrew my hand.

She took the seat next to mine, and made herself comfortable, blocking my view to the other room.

'I'm not a lesbian,' I said quickly, as she moved her hand across my back.

'No one ever is,' she said.

I looked at her, judging what was going through her head. I watched as she eyed me as well, and before I knew it her lips were against mine. I meekly pushed her away from me, but I was fairly stuck to the chair. After a few moments I stopped resisting and just let myself go. My body experienced a new sensation, one that felt right. I was lost in the moment, until I heard a slight snickering from my left side.

I broke the kiss, and looked dazedly to my left, where I found my friend watching me. She just kept giggling. I loosened myself from Shire's grip and composed myself. After a moment or so, I found that I was steady again and walked over and smiled shyly at my friend because I knew what she was thinking.

We greeted her friends and Shire, and went to the car. We drove off and on the way we started discussing what had happened.

'So how was it?' my friend asked excitedly.

'I don't know,' I said softly. I was still very self-conscious and still had to think about what had just happened. I had butterflies in my stomach and every second moment Shire would flash through my mind. The emotions I felt were still there and it felt good, which confused me all the more.

We got home shortly after midnight and I fell into bed, tired from all the thinking. There was so much going on in my head that it became difficult to dose off. An hour later I gave up trying to sleep and thought about what had happened.

My head was reeling. I was up for another two hours deciding what to do. I was confused because I felt so comfortable with being with a woman. I thought that God wouldn't punish me for being happy and following my heart. I then finally put my head on my pillow and disappeared into the realm of dreams.

As I grew accustomed to the newfound acceptance of my sexuality, I dated a few girls and never told anyone. I suspect that people knew. My aunt and uncle were constantly meeting new 'girlfriends'. I was too afraid to come out so I let them believe whatever they wanted to.

I came home one afternoon, after spending the day with a girl that I was now dating. I lazily walked into the house and was about to go to my room to take an afternoon nap when my aunt called me to her bedroom.

I huffed and headed to the main bedroom where she was watching television with my uncle. They sat there for a moment and then my aunt switched off the television. She asked me to sit down on the bed.

'What's wrong?' I asked them, my mind jumping to my father.

'Nothing,' they said together as my aunt formulated her thoughts. It was as if she had rehearsed something in her head, but was not sure if it would come out right.

'We've noticed that you bring a lot of your friends home, but none of them are boys...' My aunt waited a while before continuing. I felt that I knew where this was going and waited. I wanted them to feel how difficult it is to approach this subject. 'Are you a lesbian?' my aunt came out straight.

I waited a bit before replying because I wasn't sure how to respond. I thought about it and decided on the direct route. It was quick and painless. 'Yes, I am,' I said, finally setting their minds at ease, or so I thought.

'Oh... okay,' my aunt said, 'we just wanted to know, because

135

we reasoned that you probably weren't going to come out on your own and tell us. We thought to make it easier for you; we'd just come out and ask.'

I was so shocked by this revelation that I just stood there gobsmacked. I tried to let it all sink in, but it seemed to flow around my skull for a while before settling in.

Eventually, I laughed aloud and jumped onto the bed, feeling like a twelve-year-old again. I hugged them both tightly and told them how much I loved them and appreciated that they accepted me for who I was.

'We are not here to judge you,' my uncle said, as he sipped his tea, 'all we can do is to guide you in the right direction.'

'Don't be in too much of a rush to tell your father though,' my aunt said. 'Think about what you want to say to him and go tell him personally. Be prepared for whatever happens!'

I couldn't believe how supportive my aunt and uncle were being. *But then again, I am not their own child, so it's probably okay for them to accept me* I thought to myself.

We spent the rest of the day discussing why I didn't want to tell them. Much later I went to my room and started thinking about how I was going to approach my dad. He had already gone through a lot of pain since my mother's death. He was also just recovering from his excessive drinking and was back to his old religious self.

Back at work the following week, it became really busy. It was holiday season and tourists were flocking in to go on safaris, trips along the coast and visits to Robben Island. A woman came into the agency with her family to book a trip. Our eyes met and I turned away quickly, embarrassed that I was staring. She smiled.

'Good day,' I said. She put a few pages on my desk, described where she'd like to go to and enquired as to the best package deal. I found the most suitable one and explained it to her.

'So you're taking the trip to Robben Island?' I concluded.

'Yes,' she said, 'my family and I haven't been there yet.'

She looked at me innocently as I tried to concentrate on making the booking. I was failing miserably. I had to book the same trip thrice because her presence distracted me. Eventually I finished and I handed her the tickets. She greeted and left.

'Thank God,' I mumbled to myself, and inhaled deeply. There was something about this woman that was so attractive and alluring that it was difficult not to want to be with her.

I went out for lunch and spotted the same woman sitting a few tables away from mine. Something about her was familiar. I hid quickly behind a menu and started watching her as I waited for my food to arrive. A woman was sitting with her and they seemed to really be enjoying each other's company. As she continued her conversation, she put her hand on the other woman's hand. I noticed that the other woman didn't look comfortable with this. She broke the contact, but a minute too late as I had already witnessed the entire act.

'So she is a lesbian!' my mind declared triumphantly.

I watched them a while longer, but my vision was broken by the waiter bringing my food. As I ate, my eyes kept darting to the other table. Eventually the other woman hugged the client from the agency and wanted to kiss her. She gently pushed her away and the other one left.

Clearly, public displays of affection were not a part of this relationship I giggled to myself. I then turned my attention to my food as I only had a few minutes left of my lunch hour.

While I ate, the woman came over and sat down next to me. I was surprised to see her sitting down, as I hadn't seen her approaching. I gulped down what was still in my mouth and wiped my mouth with a serviette. She smiled from across the table, and I felt the butterflies grow wings in my belly.

'Hello, again,' she said. 'Remember me? I'm Sharon.'

I nodded in acknowledgement but continued eating.

'So why were you arguing with your girlfriend?' I asked, realising that I was being a bit forward. But I felt comfortable in her presence and it felt good.

'We're just friends,' she giggled.

We continued the conversation for several more moments and then I had to return to the office.

'Would you like to come to a party at my parent's house this Friday?' she asked me, as she grabbed her purse and walked me to work.

I was a bit hesitant, especially after the last party that I attended. I wasn't into that kind of socialising. Nonetheless, I liked Sharon, so I accepted her invitation. I could also not judge her according to other people. Besides, why wouldn't I want to spend time with this woman?

As agreed, she picked me up for the party. When we got to the house the party was in full swing. The house itself was beautiful. There were only a few people there, so it was nice and intimate. I was pleased and impressed. I liked this kind of thing. I hung my coat on the rack at the door, and then followed her through the house. She introduced me to a number of new people and then took me on a tour of the house. I followed her eagerly, wanting to see more of this beautiful house. We went upstairs. She showed me her parents' room and then her own. As we entered hers, she pulled me closer and we kissed. I was lost for a moment, not expecting this, but then kissed her back.

'I just wanted to know what that would be like,' she said smiling, wiping her lips with her finger. I smiled knowingly and then pecked her on the cheek.

She led the way back down to the party. She introduced me to everyone else who had just arrived. This was when I met Nadia. She was a plain girl, with jet-black hair. There was a subtle beauty about her. She seemed to draw one in with her presence. She was not too talkative, but not too quiet. She had a minimalist way about her and I found her quite mesmerising. I was captivated from the word go. I struck up a conversation almost immediately, as I couldn't let this chance pass me by. This was unusual as I was always the one to wait for others to approach me.

It is now three years later and we are still together. The truth is, I didn't expect anything to come from our first meeting, but we just connected and eventually we moved in together. She also went with me for therapy, to help me deal with my fear of rejection and loss. She invested in me, believed in me when no one else did. We recently moved in together and now there is only one thing left to do. I have to tell my father about the new me, who I am and what I feel.

So, here I sit in the sky waiting to celebrate my new joys. The plane prepares to land. I'm overwhelmed by the thought of what I am about to do. As scary as it is, it is something I must do in order for me to truly commit to Nadia. I release a deep breath as I put my mind to rest. No matter what happens with my father today, I can go on with life knowing that I have my aunt and uncle, and Nadia.

18

So far, so good

I was standing in our front doorway one day, when I was suddenly confronted by strange feelings. This was a first for me, and invoked emotions of worry, confusion, anxiety and sadness all combined into one. I was about eleven years old.

Worry because I couldn't understand why I fantasised about boys and not girls. Anxiety because I didn't know what the future would hold if I had to marry a girl. Confusion because I didn't know what to think about what was going on inside me. And sad because I didn't have anyone to help me to make sense of what I was feeling.

Today, as a twenty-six-year-old gay man, I shall share my story with you.

The family I was born into was a very conservative Christian one; not of the type that openly discusses important facts of life and sexuality with the children. To crown this, our parents did not allow us to play with other children in the absence of adult supervision. With Mother working full-time and Granny charged with the household chores, playing with other kids just didn't happen. My sister, my brother and I spent most of our days inside the house together. Though our parents didn't deliberately keep us away from other children, they were overprotective. They cared and didn't want us to get kidnapped, hurt or in trouble.

Mother and Granny took care of us to the best of their joint ability. Everything would be in order as long as we received three square meals a day, had clean clothes to wear, and went to school and church on time. Our emotional well-being was not a consideration. My sister had her own issues and my brother had his too, therefore I didn't have anyone to talk to. With our own personal issues to contend with, none of us had the *vrymoedigheid* to approach one another. That taught me to keep things bottled up inside. Little did I know the harm it would do to my future health.

In preschool I fell in love with a cute boy in my class. I thought about him all the time, both at home and at school. I just wanted to be close to him. I never expressed how I felt towards him. Besides, we were still only six years old.

The same thing happened in Grade 2. I fell in love with a boy in my class and fantasised about hugging and peck-kissing him. Once again, I didn't express my feelings because I didn't see it as being in love. I thought I loved him like a brother. Little did I know.

I also fell in love with girls but it wasn't as intense as the sensations I had towards the boys. I thought of the 'love' for the girls as being in love because I had not heard of homosexuality and didn't even consider the possibility of a guy falling in love with another guy. After all, what would a young boy know about these things?

In Grade 3 the kids started bullying me and calling me names. *'Meisiekind'* the boys used to call me, or *'bunny'* or *'moffie'*. I could not understand why they called me these names, which were usually used for effeminate men, and I didn't see myself as such. Looking back now makes me realise how much homosexuality was a part of me that I didn't even notice how effeminate I was. Besides, those names didn't say anything about sexual attraction and because of that I never linked my 'feelings' to those names.

During break-time, the boys used to take me away from the girls and chase me around to tire me out. When they caught me they hit and pinched me until the girls came to my rescue. It became a routine. I became scared of going to school but I had to. I was too embarrassed and afraid to tell anyone about the bullying in case me acting like a girl would come out (very silly because everyone except me could see I acted like a girl).

Later, in the higher grades, the boys started beating me with their fists and kicked me in the privates. Once, some of the boys forced me into a cupboard and tried to take off my pants to see how big my penis was but a teacher came in and stopped them. Some boys even touched my privates in a sensual way in front of the girls to belittle me. The girls laughed.

'You are a shame to the male sex,' the boys insulted me.

A few girls even threatened to kill me if I continued to act like a girl when a few boys attempted to rape me in the school toilets. On that occasion, I was saved by the bell. I dressed quickly.

'I'm going to tell the principal,' I said, but they threatened to hurt me if I did. I ran past the leader of the group and into the circle of his bodyguards at the toilet door. They halted me and would not let me go unless I promised not to tell the principle. Eventually, I relented and they let me go.

When I reached Grade 7 at the age of twelve, I met a guy whom I really liked. Already in high school and two years older than me, he used to tell me that he loved me. I let him into my heart and he took my virginity. After being sexually involved with him for a while he started to beat me, insult me in front of others and call me names, yet I still allowed him to 'use' me. I felt dirty and used after he left me. I felt uncomfortable in my body when I realised that he had only used me for the sake of his personal fun. A few years later I discovered that he was actually straight and had sex with me only because he did not have girls around to do it with. I felt that I could've saved myself for someone else who really loved me. Obviously, it was too late. I had sleepless nights thinking that I might be HIV-positive because he had several sexual partners before me. Luckily, I tested negative.

On my way home on the last day of primary school I bumped into eight of my bullies. They trapped me so that I could not run back to school and I had to run towards the hill, a deserted place where many people had been killed or robbed in the past. As children, we were very afraid of the hill because our teachers and parents warned us against walking there alone. The bullies followed me and stood on top of the hill while I tried to find escape below. They started to pelt me with stones of all shapes and sizes. I was terrified because I thought they were going to kill me. A small stone narrowly missed my face. They were wild and they bragged about how well they were aiming and throwing. I was extremely scared but eventually escaped their torture.

The bullying continued at high school. Everyone in my class made fun of me and I felt pretty helpless.

'You just need to be raped by someone with a huge penis to "come right",' one girl told me. 'That will make a man out of you.'

I developed a stress-related heart ailment late in primary school and by now I was seeing the doctor every fourth Monday for check-ups and medication. I never had an answer when the doctor asked about the reason for my stress. I was ashamed about being bullied and saw it as a weakness, so I didn't talk. Sometimes, I even wet the bed, and had headaches accompanied by nosebleeds on top of the heavy heart palpitations that I received medication for.

I started to do research on homosexuality to get a better understanding of my feelings. The interesting stuff I came across helped me feel comfortable about being gay. The research helped put a name to my feelings. I started coming out to some people close to me, including my mother and sister.

'You're imagining things,' my mother said, 'because you don't have friends and hobbies to occupy your mind.' They were convinced it was a phase I was going through. I did want friends but my past experiences taught me what the results would be. Other kids would avoid me like a plague and acted hatefully towards me. As a teenager, I spent my afternoons and weekends alone – reading, watching television or listening to music and hiding from the world. I also enjoyed spending quality time with God by praying, reading the Bible, and singing praises to the Lord, which I was accustomed to since an early age. On one particular day, I asked him lots of questions: 'How come You lessen the bullying when I ask You? Why do You always help me out when I ask? But why are You so quiet when I ask about homosexuality?' Tears rolled down my face and I couldn't stop crying. I felt God's presence strongly that day. In the background, the gospel cassette played softly and when the chorus 'Emmanuelle' played, I got this strong feeling to open up the Bible at Luke 8 verse 10. I was immediately gripped by a good feeling in my heart. I stopped praying to open the Bible. It read: *'Aan julle is dit gegee om die geheime van die koninkryk van God te ken, maar aan ander bly dit gelykenisse sodat hulle kyk sonder om te sien en hoor sonder om te verstaan.'* (Some of you will know the secrets of the kingdom of God, but others will look without seeing and hear without understanding.) I couldn't believe that I had found an answer to my question because most people don't truly see, hear or understand us. I continued to cry but this time without confusion in my heart. I cried out of joy and thanked the Lord for the answer he gave me.

On Monday morning at school I could not wait to tell one of my religious-minded classmates, whom I'd already come out to. Boy, was that a mistake! I was accused of lying and told that it had to be the devil who gave me that message. In an instant I felt shattered and confused all over again. I crawled back into the closet.

'I made a joke just to get attention,' I told everyone I had come out to. They seemed relieved and happy. The devil would answer because God doesn't condone homosexuality. Since then, my relationship with God took a backseat in my life.

In Grade 11 I fell in love with a friend's cousin. The cousin told me that he was not gay and that he would beat gays up because they annoy him. But when I told him that I was gay, he remained my friend. From then on we became better friends.

We visited each other regularly and my feelings for him became stronger. Although I became upset when he spoke about beautiful girls, I accepted it. Once, however, when I was helping him with his homework he started to stare at me. I became shy. He was a good-looking guy and I was already in love with him. He kissed me that night before he went home, and told me that he wanted to do it again. I agreed. He wiped away the first kiss and kissed me full on my mouth. I went crazy with sensation when he went home. I felt so good.

Then, my sister coaxed me to invite him for a sleepover. She suspected that we shared a deeper relationship than merely being friends. The next morning my mother caught us cuddling in bed but did not say anything. Yet.

Later, when my mother saw the love bite in my neck, she became upset. 'If you don't stop this, I'm going to commit suicide!' she screamed at me. 'I'll throw myself under a train!'

This emotional blackmail and manipulation succeeded in making me feel guilty for doing 'this' to her. She also started to treat my friend badly and insulted him by making sarcastic comments.

Again, I felt terribly scared and ashamed. My boyfriend's mother was saying the same kinds of things to him. Instead of these reactions pushing us apart, we grew closer and confided in each other a lot more than before. But later during that year we broke up because I converted to Islam and he didn't like the idea. He went back to thinking that he was actually straight.

I became Muslim knowing that Islam does not condone homosexuality but believing those who told me it is the only true religion. I just wanted to be on the 'right' path because I felt like worshipping God more deeply and Islam and its rituals seemed to make sense. (I had wanted to be Muslim since the age of nine and have been through some unpleasant crises in that regard, but that is a long story on its own.)

Now, I was Muslim and still gay, but my homosexuality took a back seat because I was so interested in Islam that I almost had no time for anything else. I enjoyed learning about my new faith until the *imam* starting speaking about how sinful and accursed homosexuals are in the eyes of God. Whenever he recited *Hadith* and *aayaat* pertaining to homosexuality, I suffered anxiety attacks, becoming sick in my stomach with nervousness. I was striving hard to be as pious and God-pleasing as possible.

I left school and moved to Azaadville in Johannesburg in order to study my new religion. I wanted to become an *imam* and *hafiz* of the Quran. Things went well at first, but later my homosexuality became an issue again. The teachers said that if we are homosexual, we would eventually be destroyed. I thought that in order for God to forgive me and be pleased with me, I had to sacrifice my homosexual feelings. I promised God that I wouldn't give in to my homosexual desires and feelings.

Afterwards, I did fall in love with a few guys but they were straight and I felt that it was God's way of punishing me for my homosexuality.

By the time I die I reasoned *there won't be much punishment left in the grave and in hell.*

A guy from Thailand who studied with me found it hard to hide his feelings for me. We never had sex and never kissed but the feelings were clear and many of my classmates noticed. At a soccer match in the courtyard one evening, some Capetonian students saw me massaging his head. 'Go home,' they jeered, 'it's not good for you to be among so many guys.'

I found it difficult to relax. I was far away from home, the place where I could watch something on TV or listen to my favourite music to calm me down. The literature on homosexuality that I studied made me feel dead scared and anxious. Before long I couldn't take it anymore. The heart palpitations and cramps started again. I just had to go home.

Back home, another challenge awaited me. Christian people I knew mocked me for becoming Muslim. Fed-up, I decided that a religion that suppressed me was no good. I stopped going to mosque.

My ex-boyfriend became a part of my life again.

'I am happily "straight",' he told me. 'Just leave "this" behind... get a girl so that God won't punish you.'

'I'll try to do that,' I agreed.

Some time passed, and we fell in love all over again.

'I don't want God to punish me. I'm straight,' he said. 'I regret being with you because it feels like I 'did it' with a brother.' I reflected that we never had penetrative sex. 'The only way that I can love you is like a brother.' He was adamant.

I stormed out of their house but he stopped me. I could sense that he enjoyed seeing me so upset, like he relished how I was unable to have his affections in the same way. I pushed him away and ran. I felt this burning urge to cry my heart out. I ran as far as I could, even past my own home and cried to my heart's content. Afterwards, I went to a *maulana*, telling him that I wanted to return to the mosque. I started moving with the *Tabligh jamaat* again and spent most of my free time in the mosque like I used to in the past. I fell back again a few months later when Christian people started teasing me again for taking my new religion so seriously.

'He's mad to adopt another religion,' they laughed and gossiped in my presence.

I started a job at a factory. Muslims who worked there respected me because I always responded to their queries about religion. I had grown a beard and never removed my *koefieyah*. However, I also felt very lonely and wanted to be with a man. My co-workers thought the sun shone from my behind, but little did they know it was only the devil with a torch. I had ceased going to mosque again, and I was preaching to them.

There was a guy at work whom I fell in love with, but he was apparently straight so the friendship could not be taken further. Simultaneously, I was also at a crossroads in my life about my faith and my sexuality, and how I could merge the two. I became tired and frustrated of falling in love with guys I couldn't have, and realised how much I was missing out on as far as dating was concerned. I needed to start mixing with other queer people, a battle that had been raging inside me for quite a few months already. I just started to cry about this guy I couldn't have because I was so anxious. I broke down. The panic stunted my movement. My mother became worried and gave me a pill to calm me down. My brother took me to the doctor.

'What could cause a person of your age to have so much stress that you break down?' the doctor asked.

'I'm gay,' I blurted out, 'I cannot be myself and that's making me sick.'

The doctor remained silent for a few seconds and I thought to myself *Here we go again...*

'Sit down on the bed,' the doctor said sitting down beside me. He massaged my hands to calm me down. This shocked and surprised me. He spoke to me like a father does to a son. He told me good things about homosexuality, stuff that I learned years back but was to afraid to believe because I thought God would curse and punish me.

After almost an hour he gave me some medication that would help me relax. As I was about to leave, he stood at the door and opened his arms to give me a hug.

'I am gay too,' he said as we were hugging. 'I am still going through tough times myself.' I was so shocked and couldn't believe my ears. I left the surgery feeling good, confused and worried. Good because I got to share my problem with someone who understood, confused because I didn't know if I should come out or not and worried about where I would go from there.

A few weeks passed. I still pondered about what the doctor said, but hadn't worked out how to deal with things. I ended up in his surgery again.

'Make up your mind by thinking of how your life would be if you suppress your homosexuality. Think how your life would be if you get married to a woman and had the life people want you to. 'Also,' he said, 'think about how your life would be if you came out and live the life you desire… Think about it seriously. Don't worry about what people think but rather how you can improve your relationship with God and be your best.'

I left his surgery feeling more positive but nervous because the ball was now in my court. I had to face the issue head on and decide which road to take.

As scared and uncertain as I was, I started coming out to some people. My brother and a few others accepted me immediately and asked me why I hadn't told them earlier. I started becoming increasingly comfortable with myself as a gay person.

At work one night, a song I liked played on the radio. I felt like dancing to the music, so I did. By the time the song finished, the others surrounded me and asked me what was wrong.

'We know you abhor dancing and music,' someone said, 'it's Western and *haraam*.'

I was sick of pretending to hate things that I really loved. I felt like crying because I felt so free. I went to my sister and told her that I am gay. She already suspected that for a long time. We cried a lot.

'Try to change,' she urged me but I refused because there was no way that I wanted to go back to the hell of self-denial. Over the next few weeks I had her listen to my explanations of homosexuality, until she agreed to respect my decision and accept me for who I was. My two favourite cousins didn't believe me at first but afterwards they embraced me and told me that they loved me regardless.

During discussions about religion with my sister, I realised that scripture could be interpreted in various ways. Slowly but surely, I let go of my rigid views. I felt as if chains tied around my soul had fallen off. I felt free. The beard and the *koefieyah* had to go. I worked on improving my appearance to start looking my age and felt really pretty. I got a lot of compliments and people who never spoke to me before, now started speaking to me. I came out to increasingly more people who accepted me. I also explained my sexual orientation to the people in the factory and answered their questions. They grew to understand me and some even apologised for telling gay jokes and being rude to me when I first came out.

I finally mustered the courage to tell my mother. Torrents of tears ensued.

'Worry about what God is going to do when you die,' she said. I felt shattered and slowly started falling back again. Once again, religion became an issue and I started questioning everything all over again – from the existence of God, to why I'm here on earth. I felt angry and didn't want to fast when Ramadan came. I was looking for answers.

Should I become Christian again, or should I just forget everything and not care at all? I pondered.

Browsing a gay newspaper one day, I saw an advertisement of an organisation called The Inner Circle and decided to call them. The guy I spoke to sounded friendly, which made me relax and open up. He suggested that I might feel better if I paid their offices a visit, to meet Muhsin.

My brother accompanied me to ensure it was not a sham organisation. Muhsin spoke to me and gave me advice. I needed more and still felt like something was lacking and he provided further spiritual counselling.

'Don't be angry with God,' he said, 'embrace Him into your life.' Through his encouragement I started going to mosque again albeit only for *jumuah*.

My family, including my mother, has accepted me and they respect my lifestyle. I'm in the process of rediscovering my God and I've made the decision to improve my life. I'm grateful that God put people in the path of my life who help me make sense of what was going on in my life. I'm also grateful for my family's acceptance when I became Muslim. They could've rejected me but they didn't. They didn't really understand homosexuality but they still accepted me eventually and did not ostracise me like many other families do. I thank God for letting me break down so that I had to go to that doctor. If I didn't I might not be where I am today.

I thank God for letting me go through what I went through because it made me a stronger person. It made me realise how not to treat people and it also made me a more accepting, understanding person who tries to understand other people's sorrow.

My granny had a prayer hanging on the wall in our living-room. I could never understand it until I came out. It reads: *'Gee my die moed o Heer om die dinge te aanvaar wat ek nie kan verander nie. Gee my die krag om te verander wat ek kan verander. Gee my die wysheid om die dinge wat ek nie kan verander nie te onderskei van die wat ek wel kan verander.'* (God, give us the courage to accept the things that we cannot change, the strength to change what we can change and the wisdom to differentiate between the two.)

I'm Raoul and this is my story… so far.

19

Lost

A little girl stares back at me from the mirror. Those hazel eyes burning into mine, those familiar pupils, yet so strange to me. My eyes look at her cheek where a red hand print is etched into her skin. Her cheeks are stained with tears and dirt as I start to remember her story. My mind floods with painful past images and I start to scream.

Within an instant I jump from the leather couch and take in my surroundings. I look at my therapist and see disappointment in his face. His thin, gray hair reminds me of my dead father as he tries to disguise his disappointment. I barely hear what he says as he mumbles something, waves me away, and says that he'll see me in a week's time. I can't make sense of what happened during my session today.

I nod mutely, not knowing what to say. He had thought that I was making progress but clearly not today. I wish I was making progress because it would give me hope. I grab my jacket and head on out the door. I quickly look back at the door and then find myself on the pavement strolling back home. As I walk through the late afternoon, it becomes clear that I need to find some other way to accept what happened to me. A burnt-out old man rooted in a patriarchal society will not be able to guide the life of a lesbian Muslim. My issues are not related to me being queer, yet the therapists constantly harp on the issues that I am queer. *Are professionals not supposed to be trained to be unbiased?* I wonder as I feel the rain pelting down. I pull my coat tighter around me as the water tries to get onto my skin.

No matter how hard I try I just can't seem to make a

breakthrough. It's as if someone or something is deliberately blocking my thought processes. I switch on the heater and strip from my wet garments. After a long, hot shower, I switch on the television and flip through channel after channel. Nothing grabs my attention.

I sigh deeply as I try to relax. I empty my mind and concentrate on my breathing. I begin a meditation process that I learnt from the therapist. At least there is something that he offered that works well. I hold my breath longer than I'm supposed to. I turn red and gasp for air, which makes me convulse in a series of coughs. I lie on the floor, trying to regain control of my breathing. After a near panic attack, everything is back to normal and I sit up and hear a few cars screeching and hooting outside.

I get up and look outside. The street is almost completely clear, except for an attractive woman who is walking down the dirty street in her couture outfit. She is a strip of vivid colour in contrast to my otherwise drab and bland existence. I watch her as the rain beats against her bright red dress; she has no rain protection and the drenched dress sits tightly on her slim body highlighting her curves. A gust of wind envelopes her. I lose sight of her as she heads around the corner.

If you could concentrate for so long on that, then you can certainly concentrate on your breathing and find your inner peace I tell myself as I head into the kitchen for a glass of water. While there, I decide to grab a sandwich, then proceed to the living-room again. I switch on the television as a distraction while I'm eating, and decide that the only way to break free from my past is to confront it head on. I have done enough pussy-footing around. I need to move on. My guidance has always come from my Creator and I decide that this is where I can find my peace.

My first experience that holds me back is my relationship with my father. Or was it a non-relationship? As I gear up for my confrontation of the past, I take out my *musallah* and perform two voluntary *raka'ats* as a special *salaah* for peace and tranquillity. As I finish my *salaah* and reflect, I ask Allah for guidance with regard to my father.

My mind goes back to my family house. I see a television set, then within a moment, someone comes screaming across the room and knocks me to the side. I see the past reflecting in front of me as if it is the present.

I feel a sharp pain as I feel blood dripping down my head. I start to cry and push myself off the floor. I hear a loud thud, as everything just crashes around me. My mother lies sprawled across the floor and I start running toward the door. I feel someone tug at my hair and I fall back screaming. I look up into a hateful face. 'So you're going to be like your mother?' my father shouts at me. He spits in my face and the last thing I see is his hand stretching out and reaching for my face. I block my face and then… I'm gone.

I find myself on the floor, facing the television. My hands are still covering my face and my body is arched into a protective shell.

'What just happened?' I ask myself as I unfurl my body, and move towards the nearby couch. I feel tears on my cheeks and blood on my head where I fell against the wall. I go to the bathroom to check the damage. I am shocked by the bruising. There is a bloody bump on my head, there are bruises across both cheeks and my jaw feels stiff and swollen. I grab the first aid kit from the bathroom cupboard, and start fixing myself.

'This feels like a horror movie,' I catch myself saying aloud. 'Just like one of those scenes where a ghost comes to kill you, but no one believes you.'

I laugh at myself, but quickly stop as it makes my jaw hurt.

I DON'T UNDERSTAND THIS!!! I cry out in frustration as the blood continues to flow. The closest hospital is a few blocks away, so I start walking to it. I let go of my head for a moment and pay dearly for it. I feel the freezing wind against my open scalp. I grab hold of the scarf quickly and continue. I get there minutes later and they take me to the emergency ward immediately.

The doctor looks at my head, anaesthetises me and I am gone. I watch as everything starts slipping away and I finally enjoy being able to let go. I am soon lost to the desert of darkness, but I know it will not last.

The past has brought me to tears and I find myself sitting in *sujoed* on my *musallah*. I brush away my tears and perform two more *raka'ats* and sit in a meditative position.

Then I am back in my old room. It seems a lot smaller than before, but as I approach the mirror, I see an old face as if I am old.

I make my way downstairs and leave quickly. I am heading to my friend's house two blocks down, and I feel really nervous for some reason. I walk up her driveway and find my mom and dad there talking to her mom. I quickly hide behind the row of bushes growing alongside the driveway.

'They were,' my father says, 'I can assure you it was the two of them, in my house.' He sounds disgusted.

'But *my* Mariah would never do that,' the other woman insists. 'She goes to church, she reads her Bible; she couldn't be kissing your daughter.'

It hits me all at once: this was the day after my dad caught me with my first girlfriend. I am about sixteen, and I have been honest with myself but no one else.

'Well, she did,' he says, roughly, 'so you keep your daughter away from my house.'

I watch as my mother tails behind my dad as they head toward our house again. I feel sorry for my mother. I creep around the back and up the ladder into my friend's room. I had just climbed through the window when her mom knocks on the door. The room is empty so I quickly hide under the bed.

Her mother is not the kind of mother to go through her daughter's things but she opens the door and walks in. I soften my breath under the bed, and watch her feet move back and forth. I can hear a drawer opening and then another, some shuffling and then they are closed again. I can feel her mother moving angrily across the floor and I slowly turn my head to see where she has gone. She is standing in front of the door. I become nervous. She kneels down. I react quickly by pulling my legs up to my chest and carefully watch as her hands start under the bed narrowly missing my feet. I watch anxiously as her stubby hands move from side to side. Suddenly, I hear the door slam downstairs and I can just make out Mariah's voice from the hallway.

She is in for it now I think while I remain under the bed and her mother heads downstairs. The next few minutes consist of me under a bed listening to muffled screams from downstairs and then running footsteps coming up the stairs. I ready myself for whoever might storm through the door. I am relieved when I see Mariah's skinny ankles coming through the door. Her sneakers are scruffy as usual, but that's what I love about her. I wait for a while, just in case her mother decides to come in. When I feel sure the coast is clear, I creep out from under the bed, and sit on her bed. She is busy in her on-suite bathroom. I wait and listen to the water running in the shower. The bathroom door opens unexpectedly and I jump back, as does she. I recover first and catch her as she almost hits the floor. She flashes a smile at me, and I find myself lost again. I remember then, and only then, that the happiest times of my youth, were the times I spent with her. She was the reason I stayed alive. She was the very thing that kept me breathing. I lift her up and she quickly moves over to the door, locking it.

An innocent smile shines on her face, and silently I ask myself *What do you see in me?* But I don't have the nerve to ask it. I could never ask because I'm so afraid that she'll realise that she can do better and leave me. I am not prepared to fend for myself in this world where all I know is abuse and profanity. There was no beauty, no depth, and no reason for life until she appeared. I hold her for a moment, not wanting to let go.

She understands and holds me quietly. We stand there for what seemed like hours, and then she takes my bag from my

156

shoulders, starts undressing me, and then leads me by the hand to the shower, where she starts rinsing me off. She starts to clean me. She holds my hand now and again, and keeps her eyes on me. I feel so self-conscious and keep my gaze lowered as I have been taught to do, but I soon find myself falling into it all. I feel a sense of belonging start to grow in that shower, as if I were meant to be here with her in this moment. I kiss her on the cheek, scared to taint the moment with a full kiss. She smiles at me, and stands on her toes to kiss my head. I feel the power flowing from her, igniting me. So much love, so much energy flowing between two beings. It is an innocent but explosive cleansing encounter.

After the shower I follow her into the bedroom and find her mother waiting on the bed. She doesn't try to hide anything, and I just stand there, numb to her mother's rage. Mariah turns to me and says: 'They are going to move me to a monastery to change me, but you know and I know that I won't ever change. I love you. Although this life will not always make sense, wait for me.' Her voice was light but I could feel her pain emanating through the words. 'I will find you.'

With that, her mother grabs her by the hair and orders me to leave. I look at Mariah's eyes – they plead that I do as her mother says. I nod, and although it kills a part of me, I leave. I sob and the tears flow down my cheeks as I make peace with the loss of a childhood sweetheart.

I compose myself and perform two more *raka'ats* with the intention of cleansing myself and making *taubah* if what I did was wrong and for Allah to give me future direction. As I finish the *salaah*, I once more go into a sitting position to reflect... I am immediately back in the past.

I am heading down a staircase. I feel an electric shock run through me. I almost fall down the stairs but I quickly regain my balance. I hurry further down, but this time a worse shock hits me, and I feel myself losing consciousness. Soon I am lying on the floor with a pulsing headache. I look up, and all I can see is a pair of working boots. I am just about to pull myself up when I am kicked in the stomach again. This is my marriage.

'You think you're smarter than me?' my husband snarls at me. 'Well, who's on the floor now, huh?'

I can taste the blood in my mouth; I can feel my teeth loosening as well. My head begins to spin.

My first husband, Hassiem, with his charming looks and personality, hid a monster beneath the surface. He was always so nice, so sweet to me, but the day after we got married, his true colours began to show. I tried to find a way to leave the marriage but I didn't want to return to my parents who had beaten me because of my sexual preferences. At least here I didn't know why I was being beaten.

I feel myself being lifted off the ground and I feel my head hitting a wall. I watch as he picks up a rod to beat me.

'Please... no...' I beg him, while pushing myself away from him. 'Don't do this, Hassiem... What did I do?'

I cry, screaming for him to stop, but he just keeps pushing and pushing. I hear a vase break behind me and I feel the glass cut through my legs. This does not deter him. He grabs me by my hair and drags me to the bedroom. He throws me on the bed and slaps me.

'I'll teach you to obey me!' he shouts angrily. 'I'll show you what it means to be my wife!'

He starts unbuckling his pants, and rips my dress open. 'NO!!!' I scream. Usually I would just lie there and take it, but now my legs were bleeding profusely, my body feels as if it is about to break and I just can't bear the sight of him. He tears my dress again, and pulls me down towards him. I scream and yell for help, but none comes. My skin crawls as he places his hands on the cuts in my thigh. He rips my dress off completely. I try to slap him but he grabs both my hands and pins them to my sides. He violently takes me in a manner that no man should ever treat a woman. I try fighting against it, I try pushing him off me but he is too strong. He keeps me down on the bed with the weight of his body, making escape impossible. He continues in this manner, knocking the breath out of me. I can't cope and let out one last scream before I black out completely.

I stay there, in this dark, unchanging abyss where my memories now wrap themselves around me. The hurt they cause me is undeniable. I wish that I hadn't remembered any of this and that I had stayed as I was because the hurt was now enveloping me. I feel like a baby in a womb where no peaceful vibrations exist; everything is alien and uninviting. I feel another shock flow through me as it had before, making me realise I don't belong here. I start moving toward a light that has suddenly appeared in the distance but then feel another shock and I am blasted out of the abyss. I wake up on the examination table and wait as the figures around me come into focus. Finally, I can see everyone and I watch as they bustle around me. I looked at them with a newfound interest and realise how lucky I am to still to be alive.

The doctor looks at me with relief in his eyes and I realise that something must've gone wrong during the surgery. 'What happened?' I ask him, and watch as he hesitates.

'You almost died,' he finally says. 'Whatever happened to you almost killed you and we had to work hard to bring you back. I wish that I could give you better news but I guess the best is that you're alive,' he says finally, and helps me to stand up. He hands me one of those four-legged crutches and I walk back to my room with the nurse. I sit down briefly and let out a long sigh of relief.

I am there for a few more hours, and then the doctor finally lets me go. I watch as more patients arrive, as I am eventually wheeled out to a taxi waiting outside. I wonder what sad events brought them here. Were they possibly the same as mine?

It is finally over. I can finally move on with who I want to be. I have nothing behind me now. The past is non-existent. Allah has entered my soul, stronger than before. I bow my head as I offer *shukr* once more. I feel light and free. I sit a while longer on my *musallah* as I perform *dhikr*.

My stomach growls, but I feel too content within myself to get up and make myself something to eat. I am saturated with the power of Allah. This makes all the difference in the world and I absorb the sudden feeling of complete freedom. Why did I have to resort to terrible therapists when the answers to my salvage lie in me and my Maker? I am finally free to look at myself as a completely free woman; ready to make mistakes, but on my own terms. No parents to haunt my decisions, no husband to break me down and no therapists to put me on a guilt trip. I am a twenty-five-year-old woman ready to tackle a new life!

I jump as my doorbell rings and I register that it has already turned evening. I quickly hop over to find out who it is.

'Hello?' I ask, hesitantly.

'Is this Mariam Jacobs' home?' a woman asks through the intercom.

'Yes.' I answer. 'Who is this?'

'I have a package that you need to sign, for Miss Jacobs,' the woman says.

'A package for me?' I mutter to myself.

'Come on up,' I say into the intercom.

A few moments pass as I wait by the door for the stranger. I hear the elevator ring as its doors open. A woman's steps come clopping down the hallway. I hear her footsteps moving toward my door. I wait for the buzzer and open the door.

I stand shocked in the doorway as the woman who was in a red dress walks toward me. She is now wearing something else, equally tasteful, but dry. I suddenly realise I know her face, although I cannot place it. I watch her as she stands in the hallway. I think she notices my feelings because she smiles shyly and lowers her gaze.

'You were wearing a red dress this afternoon?' I ask, shocked by the coincidence.

She nods her head and says, 'I went to change, it was wet. I didn't realise that you would be home that early.'

Her beauty is breath-taking and I wonder to myself why she would be a delivery assistant. With this thought, I then notice that there is no package in her hands, merely a small handbag.

I find myself speechless. Her long brown hair sways to the side as she moves her head. Her face is pale in the dim lighting, but her cheeks shine pink under her fair skin.

'So, do you know who I am?' she asks. Her voice is light as honey and I fight with myself to remember where I know her from. I shake my head, still unable to recall any memories of ever meeting this beautiful woman.

'Maybe I have been at that nunnery for too long,' she says, as she puts her hands to my face. Our lips touch and everything comes back. Like a bolt of lightning all the good memories flood my head.

'Mariah!' I exclaim, as we clasp each other.

She came back for me at the most perfect moment. Now I know that everything was meant to happen. I become lost in a kiss as I greet a new relationship. My suffering is at an end as I enter a new life with the very woman who made it all bearable.

20

Cut off, but okay

Mariam was a final-year law student and was working as an intern at a law firm. She was quiet, attentive and funny, but in a reserved way. Her parents brought her up to the best of their ability. She was well schooled in Islam and she had strong moral values. Her family was very proud of her because she always scored straight As at school.

Growing up she dated a few guys until she realised that she was really attracted to women rather than to men. Her family was orthodox in their beliefs and took a while to adapt to this discovery. However, they loved her, she was an exemplary role model in the community and she was a bright and mature person, so eventually they came to terms with her sexuality. This realisation came while she was in high school and involved in community activism and human rights issues. Her parents were also activists and were especially involved in the struggle against apartheid, so they were relatively open-minded. It did, however, take a great amount of interrogation of scripture and research before they came to terms with the fact that it was okay to be queer and Muslim at the same time.

One day, Mariam ran an errand for one of the directors of the company. This was not a part of policy, but she knew him and he was a family friend. So when he asked her to deliver a parcel to his wife, she was glad to do so during her lunch break. It also gave her something to do. She also knew Zainap, the director's wife, and thought that she could possibly spend the break with her. The stationery store was just down the road, and it only took a few minutes to get there. When she entered the store, she saw Zainap standing behind the till at the counter. She was busy with a client, so she greeted her and indicated for her to wait. When she finished, they hugged and Mariam handed over the parcel. A moment later a girl came out of the back with an order for a customer. She started to say something, but then she saw that Mariam was present.

'Sorry,' she said, 'I didn't know anyone was here.'

'It's fine, I'm just dropping something off,' Mariam said quickly.

'Mariam, this is Zahra,' Zainap said. 'Zahra, Mariam. She works for my husband's firm.'

'Pleasure to meet you,' they said simultaneously and Mariam got the impression that they meant it.

Mariam excused herself and headed back to work. The image of Zahra was fixed in her mind. She was pretty, in a cute way, with hazel eyes and long jet black hair. She was not overtly beautiful, but Mariam found something very striking about her. She went on working throughout that day, but there was always something that made her think of Zahra; a ray of sunlight, a bouquet of flowers, a lovely scent.

That evening she found that she couldn't sleep because she kept thinking about Zahra. She twisted and turned, until she eventually dozed off. Although she had a restless night, she was up before *fajr*. When the sun rose, Mariam had already showered, completed her *salaah* and was ready for the day. She took of her prayer clothing, got dressed in her formal wear, ate and was out of the door by seven o'clock. She walked briskly over to the bus stop from her apartment and she got to work an hour earlier than usual. She finished what she had tried to do the previous day and checked her to-do list for the day. The morning was uneventful and she decided to get some fresh air for her morning break. She wanted some filter coffee so she went to a café close by. At the café she felt someone tap her on the shoulder and she turned around.

'I thought it was you,' Zahra said.

Mariam found herself spinning but she quickly composed herself. 'How are you, Zahra?' she asked.

'Very well, thank you,' Zahra responded as she placed her order.

They talked and then it was time to get back to the office. Zahra started work a bit late that day because she had to enrol for a course that she wanted to attend.

'I had better go!' Mariam said as she looked at her watch.

'What are you doing for lunch?' Zahra enquired.

'I don't know. Why?' Mariam asked, hiding her excitement.

'Want to have lunch at the coffee shop? I'll be paying,' she said.

'Okay,' Mariam said, 'at one.'

Zahra continued down the street. She couldn't believe this was happening. She asked herself: *What am I doing? I've never done anything like this before! Isn't it wrong? There is something against this in the Quran; my mother always told me it was* haraam.

Mariam felt happy that she was with Zahra. She had only just met her but she just felt a sense of calmness when they were together. She was not going to mention her feelings to Zahra but she was going to enjoy the lunch meeting. That first lunch meeting became a routine, and when they met, Mariam found that she was hanging on Zahra's every word. She was still young, but she knew so much. There wasn't one day that passed that they did not see or hear from each other.

After a series of lunches, they decided to meet on a Sunday and go to the beach. Neither had transport of their own so they had to leave early to take public transport. Very early on the morning of the scheduled outing, Zahra called Mariam to cancel. When Mariam asked why, she was merely told that it had to do with 'family issues'. Mariam accepted the explanation but thought that she would enquire further when they met the next day.

During lunch-time, Mariam went to the café, but no one

was waiting for her there. When she called, Zahra's mobile telephone went straight to voicemail. She was concerned and decided to go to the stationary shop to make further enquiries. When she got there, Zainap said that she had come in earlier but had requested to leave because she was experiencing 'family problems'.

'She was wearing these really thick sunglasses and didn't seem her cheery self,' Zainap explained. 'I don't know what's going on at home but I'm not sure I like it.'

The next day when Mariam went for lunch, she found her sitting there, looking as beautiful as she always did. She breathed a sigh of relief because Zahra was okay.

'Where have you been?' she asked Zahra. 'Why didn't you call me?'

'Firstly, *as-salaamu alaikum,* Mariam. How are you?'

'I'm fine, *shukran* for asking. Okay, I'm sorry, it's just...' Mariam started, 'I was worried.'

'You didn't need to be,' she said, 'I've just been sorting out a few problems with my family.'

'But then why were you wearing sunglasses yesterday and why didn't you come greet before you left?'

'I needed to get back home, and I had a headache.'

Mariam could sense hesitation in the responses and realised that she shouldn't discuss it anymore. So, they continued having lunch and soon the whole discussion was forgotten and they slipped into their usual banter.

Life continued as normal for a few months without incident. They would spend their lunch hours together and sometimes dinner. Zahra was apprehensive about inviting Mariam to her house and did not tell her where she stayed either. She also refused to go home with Mariam.

Two weeks before her birthday, Zahra didn't pitch for work, calling in to say she had 'family problems' again. Zainap sensed that something was wrong and called Mariam. Mariam sped towards the stationery store. After discussing it with Zainap, they decided to call her. Zahra's phone went directly to the voice mailbox. Zainap then tried the landline. A girl's voice answered. She asked for Zahra.

'*Is vir jou, jou gemors!*(It's for you, you rubbish!)' she heard the girl say on the other end as the phone was slammed onto a hard surface. Mariam took the phone. Zahra picked up, she was crying and a man was shouting in the background. Zahra cleared her throat, 'Hello?'

'It's me, Mariam,' she answered. 'What's going on there?'

'Nothing,' Zahra said, 'don't worry. I'm fine. I'll see you tomorrow.'

'I'm coming around,' Mariam said quickly.

'No, don't, I'm really fine.'

Mariam heard a door slam, the sound of a slap and a man screaming before the line went dead.

They decided to both go to see what was happening. Zainap searched the files and retrieved Zahra's address and asked one of the other helpers to keep an eye on the shop. They then drove to Zahra's house. Mariam tried calling as they were driving, but it went to voicemail again. When they arrived at the house, they were shocked to see paramedics, policemen and other vehicles in the road. A policeman had arrested a man and was leading him out of the house – it was Zahra's father. There were two other women and a girl in the house as well but the person who was missing was Zahra. Zainap leant through the car window and asked a policeman what happened. He was reluctant to respond so she introduced herself to him.

'I had to call an ambulance once we got here,' the policeman explained. 'A woman was beaten up and the neighbours called the police. She was so brutally hit that she needed medical care. She was bleeding through her shirt.'

The women were shouting from the house telling the policemen to leave the man alone. 'She deserved it!' the older of the women scolded in broken English. 'She's a dirty lesbian!

166

She deserved the treatment she got!' The policeman stopped her, took out his handcuffs and arrested her as well.

'The neighbours said that this has been going on for a while but couldn't do anything because every time they asked her if she was okay, or if they should report it, she'd insist that they shouldn't,' the policeman continued to tell Zainap,

'I'm glad that someone reported the incident,' he said, 'otherwise that poor girl would have gone through so many more episodes with her family. She is a lesbian and the family is Muslim, so they could not accept her for what she was. She was apparently too afraid to lose them.'

'Sexuality and religion is a funny thing,' Zainap said.

'We have a long way to go ma'am; our constitution is over a decade in existence,' the policeman said, 'we are fortunate to have specific laws against domestic violence.'

'As her employer, will I be allowed to see her in the hospital?' she asked. 'What hospital was she taken to?'

'That's up to the hospital ma'am. She's gone to Groote Schuur Hospital.'

The father was quoting from the Quran in Arabic and speaking about his rights as a citizen. He also said that Islam condemns lesbianism and everyone condoning it by taking the side of his daughter will burn in the fires of doom.

Zainap and Mariam drove to the hospital. They went to the Enquiries Section where they were directed to the relevant ward. Zahra was in the Intensive Care Unit. Only one person at a time could go in to see her. Surprisingly, although it was a state hospital, she was in a one-bed ward. The sister-in-charge explained that it was due to her critical condition and the facility was fortunately available. She also explained that she was sedated and needed to rest, so she should not be woken up. Zainap asked if she could go first and Mariam said it was fine. She went in but came out moments later crying. Mariam wanted to ask her what was wrong but she knew she wouldn't be able to handle talking.

Mariam opened the door and was lost for a moment, not being able to see anyone in the room. Then she saw Zahra on the bed by the window. She was completely surrounded by tubes with water, with blood, and some other things that Mariam didn't know about. She felt her throat contract as she stepped closer to the bed. The horror was unbearable. Her face was completely filled with bruises. There were cuts and scabs running like a Jackson Pollock painting across her face. Her hazel eyes were closed, but clenched in pain.

She composed herself as the sister-in-charge had advised. She stifled a scream as she thought: *What did he do to her? He's her father and he does this to her? I don't understand!* And then the tears started rolling down her cheeks as she imagined what Zahra must have gone through at her home. When she went back outside, she found Zainap lost in her own thoughts but she had stopped crying. The tissue that she held in her hand was soaked with tears.

'I can't believe that man did that to sweet, little Zahra!' she said, still in her own world.

'I can't either,' Mariam said, 'he is a monster!'

'Don't ever judge people,' she said to herself. 'No matter what they do, no matter what they say.'

She hugged Mariam and they were both crying for a moment, and then she pulled back and said, 'You must support your girlfriend to the best of your ability.'

Mariam just looked at her without comment. She was still seeing the images of Zahra.

'Don't look so surprised,' she smiled, 'there are certain things that you can't hide, no matter what. I've known about you for some time, although she hasn't told me herself. As for you, I noticed it the first day you walked into my shop and laid eyes on her.'

'But we're not dating,' Mariam said, softly.

'All it takes is one of you to make the first move, plus I think you just have.'

'I'll tell my husband what happened and let him know that you need some time off for "family issues",' she smiled. They shared one more hug and then she left.

She readied herself, dried her tears and entered the room again. This time Zahra's eyes were relaxed and Mariam felt slightly at ease; maybe she's resting peacefully.

Mariam stayed there that night, and the following day. The nurses didn't insist on visiting hours because the police had told them that it didn't apply to this patient. The only time Mariam went home was when she needed to change and Zainap insisted on driving her, even though she could have caught a taxi.

A few days had passed and Zahra was starting to heal but the scars would never really disappear.

'This was necessary, Zahra,' Mariam said softly. 'Can you see that? Do you see that you could have died and all you were worried about were the values of your family? Yet, they were beating you to bits? I understand what loving your family is like, but there is a line that you need to draw. Even your manager was worried that you didn't say something before. She was crying her heart out because of what you look like. That is what you call love, Zahra. What I feel for you is what you call love and yet you want to die for a family that does not really show you this love?'

During this speech Zahra turned to her, lifted her hand and put it over Mariam's mouth. Mariam stopped because she didn't even see this happening.

'*Shukr*,' Zahra said, and then sighed heavily as if talking took a huge amount of energy. She sunk back into the bed, and continued to look at Mariam. 'I would never have seen the light without you,' Zahra rasped.

Mariam could see how tired she was, so she insisted that she rest and stop talking. 'I'll be here,' Mariam said.

A week after Zahra was admitted to the hospital, the doctors said that she was fit to be discharged. The counsellor said that she would be discharged into the care of her Aunt Rukeina because she was still a minor and her parents were both still in custody. She had no family ties with Mariam and Zainap, so she could not live with them. Zahra shook her head slightly and told the counsellor: 'My aunt is exactly the same as my dad.'

'There is nowhere else you can go, and if there is no way to prove it, then we have no other choice,' the counsellor explained.

'It doesn't make sense because she is eighteen next week and then she can go wherever she wants to,' Mariam said. 'Now you want to put her in a house where she doesn't want to be. I will take care of her!'

'There's nothing I can do,' the counsellor insisted, 'this is the law.'

'If your law gets this girl hurt again, then what?' Mariam asked. 'What's going to happen to her then? What if she dies this time? She's gone through an ordeal and you expect her to have to go into another home where her family cannot accept her sexuality.'

'My hands are tied,' she said again.

'It's unacceptable,' Mariam said as she walked out the door.

She spoke with the doctor outside and explained something, and he nodded, then they both came back in.

'I'm sorry, Zahra, we need to keep you for further observations,' he said. 'We need to make sure that the tests are all accurate, so I'm afraid you'll have to stay here for another week.'

The day of her eighteenth birthday, Mariam and Zainap fetched Zahra from the hospital. They went to Mariam's flat. Mariam and Zainap's families were also there to celebrate the birthday.

When everyone left, Zahra went to sleep in the guest bedroom and Mariam in her own room. Mariam fell asleep almost immediately because she was finally happy that Zahra was safe. They were lost in dreamland. Finally, Zahra was home. She was cut off from her family, but it was okay. She now had a new family where she belonged.

When she turned twenty-five, Zahra proposed to Mariam. Mariam accepted. They set wedding dates and it took six months to plan, although it was only a small wedding. Their colleagues were all invited because they knew that they were now family.

21

Two heads, one tale

Joe took Almaz along to the hospital for moral support. They smoked a joint along the way and he was feeling just a tad bit gutsier. Almaz knew all too well what Joe might encounter and she wasn't going to let him face it all by himself.

Joe had known Almaz since he was twelve years old. Back then, Almaz was already married at twenty-three, with two small boys. She had been the coordinator of a children's group to which he belonged. He and Niven, one of the other boys in that group frequently visited Almaz throughout their youth. The three had become good friends as the years flashed by, and the boys were now considered part of her family. Joe calls Almaz his *fag hag*, a title she proudly carries. The loyalty they share is something most people could only hope for.

Almaz had two sons, whom both Joe and Niven enjoyed being pretend parents and big brothers to. Joe also enjoyed a good relationship with Almaz's husband, Fahiem; a typical testosterone pumped male who had his own prejudices, bordering on homophobia, Fahiem had completely converted his opinion after Joe's coming out two days after his eighteenth birthday. Almaz had finally broken down that closet door and drew him out in that same blunt manner with which she dealt with most things in life. He had known that they suspected all along but he never had the courage to declare that he was gay. With acceptance and non-judgement from those who mattered most, his self-esteem improved to a level that others might assume to be vanity. Even Fahiem had in time become an advocate of gay rights in his own way.

Because of their closeness, people often assumed that Niven was also gay. Their relationship always attracted people's attention. Mostly, they moved in the same circles and attended the same functions. Individually, each was a crowd puller, and women inevitably sought Niven's attention within minutes of arriving at a party. On the other hand, Joe danced uninhibitedly, with every part of his body gyrating to the vibrations and sounds of the music.

'Your eyes are your most erotic feature when you dance,' Almaz frequently commented. 'The dark seduction of your eyes draws people closer to you.'

Niven, more of a talker than Joe enjoyed adapting his personality best suited to the company he found himself in. Typically Virgo, Joe was organised whereas Niven's Gemini traits were a cause for irritation. Joe crassly describes Niven as being half Gem, half Ni.

Joe knows that many people consider him to be conservative. He sometimes wonders about this analogy of his personality, given that he is a weed-smoking, trance and hard house fanatic who loves to party. One of his biggest vices was a fetish for good clothes, and he supposed that his generally impeccable appearance and the reserve with which he dressed for work influenced this assumption. He never skimped on the cost of clothes if he knew he looked good in something. Besides, he was now able to afford the luxury, and the holiday breaks he indulged in occasionally. He had been the national administrator of the Children's Movement, which he had grown up in for three years, but eventually opted to have a go at the corporate world. Now, he was working at an international travel agency. The salary and perks were good, and he often travelled to some of the Western Cape's finest resorts and hotels to rate their services. He acknowledges that his life is damn good as it is.

At present, his love life was positively dormant. Sometimes he experienced serious bouts of depression. Thankfully these periods did not last too long because his closest friends supported him through his mood swings. But his friends, colleagues and Facebook networks didn't always make up for the absence of a partner.

Joe had learned that the gay world had many double standards, as if being gay did not come with enough challenges to deal with. Part of his reason for following a vigorous fitness regime and taking such immaculate care of himself was because one could never be too thin or too beautiful in the three-dimensional gay society.

There was never a shortage of suitors, but Joe was finicky. Though he did not have a problem with older men, he wasn't prepared to get hung up on someone who would most likely die before he did, let alone lacking the stamina to keep up with his lifestyle. He knew this sounded really callous but that's just how it was for him at this point in his life. Besides enjoying a good party he also ran up and down Table Mountain every Sunday. No, he was definitely not seeking the sugar-daddy type who thrived on the thrills of orgies and kinky sex. Perhaps he was too much of a romantic to consider the underworld side of some gay lifestyles. Ideally, he wanted a life partner; maybe even adopt a child or two. He wanted love, and at twenty-five he supposed he was just being idealistic. Nevertheless, he was confident that he usually managed to get what he wanted if he put his mind to it...

They sat in the car, in the hospital parking lot for at least ten minutes before Almaz managed to spur him on to finally get out of the car. Inside, she took a seat on one of the benches just outside the ward.

About half a dozen or so people, wearing customary Islamic attire, were already in the ward where his father was convalescing. He stood in the doorway for a while, not wanting to disturb the Quranic recital being intoned by his older brother Junaid. His mother sat on the bed, holding his father's hand, her head bowed slightly. His father's aunt Amatie was seated at the foot-end, rubbing her nephew's feet through the white hospital sheets. Both of his sisters and their spouses were also in the ward. At the far end of the room near the window he noticed his cousin Nawaal, who winked to acknowledge him. He was glad to see she had come. They had been quite close as kids but rarely saw each other these days. The technology of cellphones and computers, however, ensured that they maintained regular contact. Nawaal was the only link he had with his family, and it had been her who had informed him of his father's grave condition.

'*Amien,*' everyone softly chorused as the evening's recitation concluded. Joe stepped into the ward and collectively everyone looked up. His mouth was dry and his tongue stuck to his palate.

'*As salaamu alaikum,*' he managed hoarsely. The response was a barely audible mumble, except for Amatie who appeared almost pleased to see him. He didn't bother to greet the men with the Islamic hand-shake, nor to kiss-greet the women. He had been rebuffed too many times before. His was a case of many times bitten, purposefully shy. He took a few steps towards the bed and greeted his unconscious father by kissing him on the forehead.

'S*alaam,* Daddy. It's me... Yakoeb,' he murmured.

At least the family members gathered there had the decency to leave him alone with his dad for the next few minutes before visiting time finished. He sat on the chair next to the bed and took his father's weathered hand. He studied the hand carefully, reading in its creases and scars the hands of a once hardworking man. Joe looked at his father's face and realised just how much he had aged since he last saw him over five years ago. His eyes stung a little as a melancholic mood set in.

'When did you become an old man, Daddy?' he asked quietly. 'You've always been one of the strongest men I know... and despite everything that's been said and done, I want you to know that I've always respected you. I'm so sorry that I disappointed you...' Joe cleared his throat. 'It is not for me or for you to forgive. I want you to know that even though I was angry with you for a while, I understand the issues better now. I hope that you also got to understand me a bit better. *Shukran* for everything...' He got up, kissed his father's hand and departed.

Three days later just after *jumuah*, Joe got into his white VW Fox and turned on the radio. It was still tuned to the local Muslim radio station, as he had listened to parts of the lecture as he drove to the mosque earlier. He caught the last bits of a *janaazah* notice being read by the female announcer. She repeated the notice as if courteous to his needs and his stomach lurched violently as he heard the name of the recently deceased. 'Aghmat Salie,' the announcer said again, 'aged 63, passed away after a short illness. Junaid Salie can be contacted on his cellphone for further details. May the departed soul be granted *Jannatul Firdous, Insha-Allah.*'

He switched off the radio and was suddenly overcome with unexpected sadness. He sat in stunned silence trying to make sense of the loss he felt. His cellphone's cheerful ringtone abruptly interrupted the hundreds of thoughts he seemed to be having all at once. It was Nawaal, informing him of his father's death. He was lighting up a Camel Light when his phone rang again.

'Where in the hell are you?' his manager, Ausla, from work wanted to know. He checked the time and realised it was almost an hour past his lunch-time. Joe apologised and explained. Ausla sympathised and insisted he take the rest of the day off as well as a few days leave if he needed it. Joe often reminded himself just how fortunate he was to work at a place he liked and the gem of a boss he knew he had. He started the car and headed home.

Joe had no intention to attend the *janaazah*. No one would expect him to, he supposed.

Almaz lived two houses away from him. He had spent most

of his life in this very area until his family moved to Rondebosch eight years ago. Almaz had persuaded her widowed neighbour, auntie Kia, to let the extra room in her house to him shortly after he left home. Joe parked and popped in to visit Almaz first, as he did every day after work. He found her in the kitchen chatting to Niven who had also stopped by after college.

'You're home early,' Almaz observed.

'Hey *bru*,' Niven extended his hand in greeting.

'What's up? You looked perturbed,' Almaz commented.

'Just heard my dad's dead,' he blurted after a brief pause.

Almaz and Niven looked at each other, not sure what to say. Niven spoke first: 'And how you doing?'

'Please Niven, don't go analysing everything. I'm fine. Okay?' Joe snapped unintentionally.

'I think we both want to know if you're okay Joe. You look like crap,' Almaz intervened.

'I'm a bit rattled, which I find… shocking, given the circumstances…' he trailed off heading in the direction of the backyard, dubbed 'The Green Lounge' by its usual patrons.

'Anyone wanna join me for a blessing?'

After they smoked the joint in silence, Almaz asked if he would be attending the *janaazah*.

'You are obviously very stoned to be asking me this crap,' he responded, an expression of disbelief on his face.

'No, I'm serious. I think you should go,' she said ignoring his condescending attitude.

'I agree with her. You owe your old man at least that.'

Almaz glared at Niven. Sometimes he could be extremely tactless and she would end up doing damage control. Joe's eyes narrowed at Niven and his lips curled into a sneer.

'I'll go along if you want,' Almaz added hastily.

'No! *Nancy*! *Nee!* What's wrong with you people?' he glared at Almaz. 'Weren't you the one who pointed out the other night that there was no way they would welcome back the queer, prodigal son? I mean… you were there man! You saw how they ignored me. I'm no longer one of them... haven't been for a long, long time. Can we leave it at that?'

Almaz was not easily put off. 'I know your reasons Joe, but I also know you. It won't sit well with you if you don't go. Prove to them that you are more than what they think of you,' she squeezed his hand. 'It's one's final duty to those who raised us, babe.'

'I hear what you are saying. It's just that I'm so freaked out... and tired of being rejected over and over again,' he sighed. 'But yeah, I suppose you are right. I should go.' He looked at Niven. 'And you have given your take, so I guess majority rules?'

'Yep. But we won't make you go to Faieza's when it's her time, okay?'

Joe went home to cleanse himself as was required for a Muslim burial. After completing the *janaazah ghusl*, he dressed and donned a black thobe and fez. Almaz arranged with Niven to baby-sit, and to inform Fahiem of what was happening when he returned home from work. Nawaal had mentioned earlier that the body would leave the house shortly after *maghrieb*, the sunset prayer.

'Are you sure you don't want me to drive? You look like a strangled chicken with that scarf tied so tightly under your chin,' Joe joked in the car.

'*Ya nay*... the things I have to do for you,' she smiled back.

They parked on a small field opposite the house. Both sides of the street were lined with cars.

'My dad's adoring fans till the end,' he mused.

'He wasn't all bad Joe,' Almaz, the eternal optimist, reminded him.

They watched as a silver-grey Chrysler arrived.

'Mmm... posh *ne*? Who's that?' she asked watching an elegant middle-aged couple getting out of the car. Joe tried to get a better look, but it was the man's walk he recognised first. Almaz turned, wondering why he had suddenly gone quiet but immediately made the connection.

178

'Oh, my god! It's him!' she exclaimed softly. Joe seemed transfixed.

'Yoh! Look Joe, I'll understand if you want to leave right now.'

'No. We've come this far and I'm sure as hell not turning back because of him!'

Almaz's guilt grew fast. What was she thinking convincing him to come here? How could she have been so insensitive to all the hurt her friend had endured in his life with these people?

'You and your damn good intentions Almaz,' she muttered under her breath.

'It's okay hun... I've got this one.'

He opened the car door, got out and stuck his head back in.

'Are you coming?'

The smell of spices, camphor and incense sticks greeted them as they neared the gate. Small children chased each other about on the front lawn and despite several warnings from the adults, they were quite rowdy. The green burial panel-van was parked in the narrow driveway. They exchanged sombre greetings with the people congregating outside the house. He felt some relief that they had not passed a familiar face yet, but he knew it would be short-lived.

'What now?' he whispered to Almaz, 'do I wait outside or go inside to *ziyaarat* my father?'

'*Salaam* you two. I knew you would come,' Nawaal hugged and kissed them both. 'I figured you could use some help braving the elements,' she smiled, gesturing towards the expanse of people he would be encountering.

'I suppose the worst thugs are inside,' Joe said as she led them in.

A group of women stood in the doorway and the trio greeted as they passed.

'That's Yakoeb, the one who became a *moffie*,' he heard one of them whisper as he stepped inside. He turned his head slightly to see who had spoken. 'Are you sure it's him?' another asked.

179

'He doesn't look queer at all.' To make sure that it was in fact him, the first speaker repeated his name a bit louder and he turned around instinctively, feeling somewhat stupid when he realised what had just happened. He gave them a sugary smile.

'Oh yes, I had almost forgotten that I'm going to have to call you Yakoeb for now,' Almaz said smiling.

'Don't you dare do anything to win their favour,' he responded with a serious tone.

Joe was in no way embarrassed of his name but he had decided shortly after his family disowned him that he would also lose the identity related to them. 'Joe' was often used as a pet name to shorten 'Yakoeb'. Of course his family believed – as most Muslim families did – that it was un-Islamic to address a child by anything other than their name given at birth. Joe had given up trying to win popularity contests over it with his family. Their opinions on anything he did had ceased to matter a long time ago. Everyone these days knew him as Joe and he was accustomed to getting the 'But that isn't a Muslim name, is it?' from those who learned he was a practicing, even devout Muslim. In more ways than one, he knew all too well that becoming Joe was possibly the biggest form of rebellion against his bigoted family. His other vice as rebellion was resorting to smoking marijuana.

The house was filled to capacity. People sat or stood anywhere they found some space. Amatie was seated at the passage entrance, directly across the room where the body of her nephew (whom she had reared since the age of three) lay. Her tiny creased face was red from silent weeping. Joe bent down to peck her on the cheek. Her usual twinkling eyes seemed to have lost all their mischief. Amatie was the one person who briefly hugged him before he stormed out of his parents' home that horrible day five years ago. 'Leave, my child. You will be better off anywhere else but here,' she had whispered. Joe had always respected her mature wisdom.

'How dare you show your face here?' He heard his sister Soraya's voice. He turned to face her. *Opponent number one* he mused.

'*Salaam*, Soraya. Nice to see you too,' he smiled.

'Don't talk crap to me!' she said quietly enough to be considered a whisper.

'*Ya Allah* Soraya, where are your manners? It is our *buya's kifaiyat*,' he responded in a similar tone of voice.

'Don't joke around Yakoeb. Do you want Mommy to have a heart attack and also die when she sees you here?' her face showed that she shouldn't have asked the question.

'Do you really think that it could happen that easily, hmm? Now why didn't I think of that one?' he teased.

Soraya knew better than to continue. She glared at him then stomped off.

'Shame, poor Soraya's nerves are shot now,' Nawaal feigned concern.

He entered the room in which his father lay. The body lay stretched out on the bier, completely prepared for burial except for parts of his face which were still uncovered. The room was filled with men. Except for a few curious stares in his direction, no one said anything. He managed to see his father's face and paused for a few moments to look at the quiet face of the man who had raised him. Aghmat Salie had ensured that each of his children received the best education he could afford and equipped them with a vast knowledge of the *deen*. Joe had learned generosity as well as anger from his father. He recalled the anger part all too vividly.

One such time was on his eleventh birthday. His father and uncle had taken him, Junaid and two of his friends on a camping trip to Ceres. Joe had been too shy to remove his swimming trunks in front of the others. Junaid and his buddies started teasing him, calling him a girly-boy. His father, perturbed by his youngest son's behaviour broke off a branch from a nearby tree and started hitting him. He did not stop until Joe's legs, parts of his back and arms were bleeding and covered in thick, angry welts.

Later that evening his dad and the other three boys went to

collect some twigs for the fire. Joe had cried himself to sleep after the beating and had woken when it was already dark. Alone in the tent, Joe finally removed his swim trunks and was wiping sand from his crotch which had started to itch, when his uncle ducked in. He accused Joe of being a perverse *shaytan* and threatened to tell Faieza when they returned home. Joe feared the devil less than he did his mother. Joe had wondered what it was that he had done to upset his uncle so much. All he remembered was his uncle telling him how boys who wanted to be *moffies* had to be dealt with.

He started to leave the room when, as fate would have it, he practically knocked heads with the uncle in question. They both started to apologise before looking up. Only his close friends knew of his abuse. And so did his dear uncle Faiek whom he was now facing for the first time in over nine years. After the incident this very same uncle would always look at him in this exact questioning manner. His face always seemed to ask: 'Have you told yet? You wouldn't dare would you, perverse little *shaytan*?' There seemed to be something else he recognised in addition to that look now. His eyes showed fear. Someone squeezed past, interrupting the awkwardness and Joe walked away.

He spotted Almaz in the dining-room and got her attention by waving.

'Guess who I just spoke to?' Almaz whispered. Joe raised his shoulder and she continued putting her mouth close to his ear. 'Gouwa Majiet. *Moulana* Ashraf's wife,' she added when he shrugged.

'Oh! Geisha Ashleigh?'

'Sshh. Not so loud,' Almaz quickly scanned to see who might have heard. 'Yes… the one and only. Apparently they are *talaaqed* and she and the kids now live in Wynberg.'

'Don't worry about who heard me, that one's a total undercover *Mavis*. I doubt if Gouwa even knows he's gay. I mean my gaydar didn't even pick up that one, nor did yours for that matter and you're *gooood*. If it wasn't for Adam's party and I didn't actually see him dressed as a geisha, gyrating with the apprentice *Mavis*'s, I don't think I would have believed it. That's how good he is.'

'Well, I'm sure she does know by now. Why else did they split up then?'

'What are the two of you *fitna-ing* about?' Nawaal asked as she joined them. 'Tell me later,' she added. 'Your visit has caused quite a stir around these parts, so I'm going to take you two to my place in the back. Hang on tight, this might be a rough ride.'

She ushered them out the back door, through the kitchen where about ten women were preparing food and piling paper plates with small pies, samoosas and spring rolls.

He recognised five of them; two aunts and three cousins. The others were probably neighbours or from Faieza's ladies *jamaah*. He greeted as they passed. He hadn't seen Faieza yet, who he assumed to be in her bedroom being comforted by Junaid and Shehaam, his eldest sister. He had also not seen them yet. But as they exited the kitchen he noticed them immediately, huddled together, comforting their mother in the backyard leading to Nawaal's separate entrance. The two women winging him had not yet noticed the trio and Nawaal kept talking.

'How long have you been staying back here?' Almaz asked Nawaal.

'I've been here for just over a week now. Some of my things are still unpacked so forgive the mess. I didn't expect a *janazaah* a week after moving in.'

Junaid was first to look their way and came towards them.

'Leave now!' he ordered, anger written all over his face.

'I'm at my father's *janaazah*, the same way you are. But don't worry, I won't be sticking around for much longer,' Joe replied coldly.

'I want you to leave right now. Don't you have any skin on your face man? Or are you hoping to get some inheritance now, after all this time?' Junaid continued spitefully.

'Oh, there's no need to concern yourself about that, *boeta*. I would never dream of impoverishing the rest of you like that,' he bit back flashing Faieza and Shehaam a smile.

Junaid looked as if he might explode at any minute.

'I've invited them to have some tea with me and then I'm sure they'll be leaving, what with this wonderful welcome they've received so far,' Nawaal chipped in. She took their hands and led them away.

'Do you know of a place I can rent 'cos I'm sure as hell gonna need it after that disobedience,' she laughed as they stepped inside.

The little cottage built at the back of the main house had not changed much since he had last seen it. The walls were still the same vomit green. He noticed the gold-framed *rakam* to his left: 'And hold on tight to the rope which Allah stretches out for you and be not divided amongst yourselves' it read.

How ironic, Joe thought. In this family one's hands were beaten free from that rope if one were thought to be in any way a disgrace to the revered Salie or Latief name. He looked around and only vaguely heard Nawaal tell Almaz to keep her company in the kitchen while she made tea. In the far corner of the room he noticed some familiar items of furniture that were probably being stored away in the room or perhaps they had allowed Nawaal to use. He moved up close for a better look at the antique chest that had once stood under the stairs in the main house. Still covered with a thick piece of glass, it now had a thin hairline crack running down the middle. Underneath were the same photos he remembered since childhood. Photos of his dad and Faieza on their wedding day, and then later on *hajj*. An old black and white picture of Amatie as a young woman, walking down Adderley Street, christening photos of his siblings, beach outings, picnics... The vacant spots indicated that some photos had been removed. No prizes for guessing which ones those were, he thought with a twinge of bitterness. There were no half measures with these people.

He sat down on the bed and tried remembering some of the good times in this place he once considered home. However, the first memory was one he thought had been long buried in the past, and one of the reasons he saw a shrink.

It was in this very room that his parents, brother, both sisters, their husbands, the local imam and three *tablieghis* had 'ambushed' him. He knew that his family had suspected he was gay but had begun to think that they were in some strange way starting to accept it. He even naively concluded the reasons for their 'acceptance' as a preferred method to hide behind ignorance instead of risking their unblemished status.

He had to admire the imam's bluntness of approach.

'Your family is concerned by whether you are homosexual,' he had come straight to the point. Oh, how Joe hated that word. After years of battling with his sexual identity, growing up in a staunch Muslim home and educated according to the laws of *Shariah* he was finally allowed the admission because he was asked. He heard his mother's disbelief at his honesty.

'*Astaghfirullah*!' she sounded so shocked that he wondered at the extent of their concern to organise this ambush. Shehaam had started crying and his father turned his back on him. The *tablieghi* whose heads had been bowed all this time now openly stared at him with complete distaste. They reminded him of the three hyenas in the Lion King, greedily awaiting the imam's words of dogmatic wisdom. He awaited the much quoted reference to Prophet Lut (Lot) and the decreed punishment for homosexuality according to *Hadith*. The imam however, surprised him with a different approach.

'Many modern Muslims justify indecent, mischievous and sinful acts by convenient interpretations of the Quranic text. Are you one of those who show rebellion and arrogance towards our Creator, Yakoeb?' Joe's *imaan* and *taqwa* were being attacked. He looked at the three hyenas, waiting for him to crack under their learned and intellectual leader.

'I am a Muslim before I am anything else, Imam. Why do

my own judge me so severely about something I never chose to be, much like a parent who doesn't have the choice of a preferred sex for a baby they await? Are you thus questioning God's creations or are you just naturally bigoted? Do you also judge our Creator for making people of different colours or those born with defects? Just how deeply rooted are your prejudices towards the One who is oft forgiving and most merciful? That is what you are suggesting aren't you, Imam? That I make lots of *taubah* in order for this affliction to be removed?' Joe had never before needed to defend himself about being gay like he did that day. The words he had spoken had come from the most sincere parts of his being, which left him feeling drained and light-headed afterwards.

'What's wrong with you?' It was Junaid's turn to rile him. 'You've got no shame standing in front of your parents and imam and admitting that you're a bloody homo. You have obviously lost *al-Adaab* man! Allah doesn't make homosexuals! It was your *choice*!' Junaid emphasised the last word.

'Can we attempt to council the boy without shouting?' the imam intervened, looking a bit flushed.

His mother ignored the imam. 'I've known all along... since Aghmat insisted we take him from that low-life whore of a mother of his, that he would be bad news...'

'Faieza! Stop it right now,' his father demanded. Joe's head was spinning, no longer sure if any of this was really happening.

'No Aghmat!' Faieza shouted, spewing saliva. 'This is the last straw. I will make it known today that no child of mine will cause such shame. He is your punishment for committing adultery,' she spluttered.

Silence had never been that deafening. Joe felt as if he were falling, swirling down a dark well at a slow, painful speed. He looked around the room. Everyone else except Faieza and the clergy seemed to be caught in the same dark well of shock. After what seemed like an eternity, his father finally broke the spell by quietly walking out. He realised his eyes were stinging and he

186

was unable to swallow back the lump that suddenly appeared, threatening to choke him. He followed a few moments later feeling as if he had just been stripped of everything he believed in, trying but unable to fathom how his life could be changed so drastically, yet so simply, within minutes.

He paused at the door on his way out, started to say something and hesitated. 'Yes I am gay. And I wonder if I would ever have learned the truth if I was not,' he looked at the woman whom he had believed was his mother for nineteen years of his life. 'You probably would have sooner or later. You've obviously been dying to get that off your chest, haven't you?' he cleared his throat. 'Maybe now I can accept why my mother hated me so much...'

When he looked up, he noticed Almaz and Nawaal at the door's entrance, silently watching him. He realised he was crying.

'Let's get out of here,' Almaz reached for his hand.

He realised that his day was not going to end on that grand note when he saw the matriarch and her family enter the kitchen as he prepared to leave. Nawaal stepped between them.

'Please don't cause any drama. He is on his way out anyway.' Faieza ignored her and stormed directly towards Joe, slapping him across the face. 'How dare you show your face here after all the shit you put my family through?'

Joe didn't want to deal with anything right then and stepped past her. Junaid grabbed him by his arm and pushed him aggressively. Before Joe could think logically, he punched his brother hard enough for him to go sprawling. He saw the brief look of disbelief on his brother's face before another hand grabbed him from behind. Faieza again. He shrugged her off as Junaid lurched towards him once again. This time, it was Joe who got punched squarely in the face. Dazed, he heard women screaming. He tasted blood and realised his nose was bleeding. *No way, this little rubbish didn't just break my nose, did he?* Joe thought amidst all the madness. *Deal with the war injuries later*

Joe he thought. *Time to wrap this up*. Junaid came for him again and tried knee-butting him in his stomach but Joe was ready this time and stopped any impact by extending his entire leg, catching Junaid unintentionally in the groin. His brother fell back groaning in pain. Faieza dramatically dropped to her knees at her son's side and Almaz produced tissues to dab Joe's nose.

He noticed that they had attracted quite an audience, most of whom looked shocked and a few of the women were crying. A frail voice penetrated the chaos, demanding they stop immediately. It was Amatie, slowly making her way towards him. The old woman handed him a handkerchief before addressing the crowd in a voice breaking with emotion.

'I am so disappointed in everyone here,' she said focusing on Junaid and his mother, still crouched on the ground. 'My child is not even in his *kabr* yet and you have all disrespected him already. The saddest part of all is that this happened because his son had enough respect to come to his daddy's *kifaiyat*... Don't you think that you have caused him enough hurt already?' her voice broke and she started weeping. Two men led her back inside and soon the crowd followed, leaving Faieza and the others to compose themselves.

Only when everyone was inside did Joe notice that Faieza's brother Faiek was standing next to his sister, trying to comfort her. He so much wanted to leave, bury the happenings of today along with his dead father until Faiek opened his filthy trap.

'Once again he has managed to bring shame and disgrace. None of this would have happened if he just stayed away.'

Joe felt his ears burning, the top of his head tingling with an electrifying heat. Hurt and anger collided and before he could suppress anything he heard himself bitterly retaliating with a voice that was even and calm. 'You are all so judgemental of a tainted existence. Yet it is your damned family who is consumed with enough hatred to set off a nuclear explosion. Then he said, pointing at Faiek, 'You stand here and actually have the gall to talk crap when it was you who raped me on my eleventh birthday.' Faiek went deathly pale and Joe briefly wondered if he was having a heart attack. 'Your own brother... pure, unadulterated Latief blood!' Joe said addressing Faieza. That said, he walked away, not in the least interested in whatever would unfold.

Almaz had started the car and they were just about to drive off when Nawaal came running towards the car, gesturing that they wait.

'Just before your dad went into a coma, he asked me to ensure you get this,' she handed him a brown A4 envelope with 'FOR YAKOEB' written across the front in red ink.

'Aren't you keen to know what's inside?' Almaz asked as they took the turn onto Vanguard Drive. Neither of them had spoken. Joe seemed to be in his own world and she didn't want to disturb him. She was a bit concerned by his lack of interest in the envelope.

'I'll read it later. I don't have the strength to deal with any more right now,' he replied in the monotone he sometimes used to get his message of 'leave me alone' across.

He turned down her offer of coffee once they got home and said he wanted to get straight into bed. He was exhausted.

'Well at least you know your nose isn't broken. In fact it's looking better already. Maybe you should have it checked out anyway. We can't have that perfect Egyptian nose damaged, can we?' she teased trying to ease the mood a bit.

'I might do just that, but tomorrow. *Salaam* Almaz and *shukran.*'

She watched as he unlocked his front door. She was more than just a little concerned for her friend.

Joe took a steaming hot shower, which provided no release from the day's events. He had thrown the envelope onto the bed and tried not to give it much thought, but as he got under the covers he picked it up and stared at his father's familiar handwriting for a while before carefully opening it.

My Dear Son,

Where do I start to tell you how truly sorry I am for all the pain you had to endure from me as your father and the unwise decisions I made in my life. Removing you from your birth mother, thinking that I was able to give you a better life with my existing family… At the time I had no idea that the woman I married would be so unforgiving and make my illegitimate child the focus of all her resentment. I will share with you my story because you deserve to know the truth.

Twenty-seven years ago, the first time I went to Iran, I met someone I had been in contact with via telephone and business letters. Her brother owned the business but she designed all the pieces herself. He admired my designs and was willing to finance some of my ideas. Once I arrived they insisted I stay with them instead of paying for accommodation elsewhere. During my two-month stay in their home, and working closely together, we all became good friends and we were all rather sad to part when the time came for me to return home. Of course, I had a family back home and an extension of my stay there was out of the question.

I did, however, return a year later and it was during this time that my friendship with Yasmin grew into something more and you were conceived. Because of the strict laws against an unwed pregnant woman in Iran, I arranged that she come to South Africa to have the baby. She stayed the remainder of her pregnancy with Amatie in Durban and I was able to visit her quite frequently. After a while I was no longer able to live with my guilt and I confessed to Faieza. I even asked that she grant permission for me to marry Yasmin but she refused. Naturally, she felt hurt and scorned. She threatened divorce and denying me any access to my other children. Two months after your birth, Yasmin, although heartbroken to leave behind her baby, had no choice but to return home. It was arranged that Amatie, with the help of a nanny, would rear you. In this way I could see you as often as I wanted. Unfortunately this arrangement didn't last too long because Amatie suffered a bad stroke. Unprepared to have my son adopted by others, I brought you and Amatie home. You were five months old by then and I allowed Faieza no option. She was reluctant but had to accept it, with the condition that people were made to believe that you were adopted. This saved her the embarrassment of letting others know, at the same time making her seem even more pious and good-hearted.

I became your main care-giver until you were about four, when the expanding business meant I often had to travel. Faieza suffered depression for many years, the main reason being my special love for you. She believed that I was unfair to your siblings, and knowing this to be true, I hardened myself to most things in life, including you.

You had always been an extremely well-mannered, quiet child and by the time you were about nine, Faieza accused me of turning you into a softy, a fag, she said, because of your often effeminate mannerisms. I had already noticed this and when she mentioned it, it became a concern of mine, making it almost easier to be harder on you – toughening you up, I thought. The rest as they say is history.

As for Yasmin… we have always stayed in contact. Perhaps you can recall the time you were twelve and I took you to Pretoria for the weekend. The woman we had lunch with was your mother who so badly wanted to see you. Faieza somehow found out about this 'reunion' and threatened to expose Yasmin 'for the whore she is'.

Your mother has always wanted you to be a part of her life which has been difficult until now. Perhaps my own cowardliness played a huge role in this restriction but there is nothing more that prevents you from making contact with her now. My last wish is for you to consider it. Enclosed you will find the necessary information which will make your meeting with her as convenient as possible.

Lastly, my beloved son, I ask for your forgiveness for the mistakes I've made concerning you. I know that the inheritance I leave you could never make up for all your pain but I'm hoping that it will make your life easier. I've preempted your stepmother's and siblings' reactions to this and have therefore also included the legal documentation making you the primary heir to my business. I know you have inherited your mother's strong sense of pride and you might not accept my offering, but I ensure you that they are all equally well taken care of.

Your Father

Between the stack of five pages, Joe also found a photo of a dark-haired, attractive woman. Her eyes seemed to be a reflection of Joe's. He felt a greater connection with this simple photo than he ever had with the woman who raised him. He duplicated her smile and tenderly wiped the single tear that had fallen on the photograph. He had found an identity greater than any inheritance and he couldn't wait to meet her.

Joe got dressed and went over to Almaz.

All his friends – his other family – were in The Green Lounge and Joe took his usual seat.

'I'm sorry Joe, I shouldn't have made you go today,' Almaz apologised.

'It's all good,' he answered still not willing to show the excitement that was ready to burst.

'Damn! I had no idea your family was that messed up Joe,' Wendy continued in her tactless manner. There was a knock on the gate.

'The vibes are rather hectic in here tonight guys. Whatever it is, it can't be that bad. You know my philosophy: Crap happens, it's just the depth that varies, but we cope with it,' Shireen said, who refused to let anything get her down. Going on fifty, she looked no older than thirty-five.

'Joe's father died today Reenie,' Tara explained.

'And are you alright Joey?' she continued without skipping a beat.

'Fine,' Joe answered pensively.

'Amatie was also there,' Almaz offered.

'Wow, how old is she now?' Shireen exclaimed.

'About three days older than Moses, isn't that so Joe?' Niven responded sheepishly.

'Yoh! You are a real bastard,' Wendy joked.

'You know what's amazing?' Tara asked. Everyone waited with dramatic expectation. After a few puffs of a joint twenty-eight-year-old Tara usually became very profound. 'All of us here have had tough lives, especially with our families. We are all broken children and it's God's gift to us that we have found each other and became family,' she looked around the yard. 'This is the place we come to when the world becomes cold. Here no judgements are passed… no envy… no greed. In this Green Lounge we are all VIPs. Yippee! I'm a member! I get a front seat!' she concluded by flaying her arms above her head. Everyone smiled in quiet acknowledgment.

'And here I went spending loads of money on a shrink,' Joe exclaimed, disturbing the magic by banging his fist on the table.

With the sombreness instantly removed, Joe moved closer to the fireplace and told his story.

Joe knew that his struggles as a gay Muslim man were far from over. In a world where people's prejudices are a norm, it was a struggle he knew he would often encounter. It was never easy to convince people to change their opinions, especially when they had preconceived ideas on homosexuality. Promiscuity and child molestation topped this long list. Even in a modern society, gay men and women are killed in the most gruesome fashion by those indoctrinated by fundamentalist dogma. They use religion as an excuse to commit murder and other atrocities. Iran executed an estimated four thousand homosexuals since the revolution in 1979. Homosexuality existed long before the scriptures were revealed and it is only now, over two thousand years AD that the gay minority has stood up against being ostracised by fighting back. The struggle continues…

22

Coming Out

In my family, my spirituality as a woman is judged by two things: making *salaah* five times a day, and not wearing manly clothing. Doing anything else escapes persecution. Needless to say, when I came out as a lesbian at the age of twenty, it wasn't a big deal.

'Not another one,' was my mother's only comment.

I have a sister who was younger than me when she came out, and I have another older sister. I was the last one, and therefore the last disappointment. My father didn't really mind because he just wanted us to be happy.

Let me tell you a bit about him. My father is the kind of man who would help a stranger off the streets. When my cousin fell pregnant, her mother hid it from the world. My aunt forced my cousin to endorse documents to have the child adopted at birth, but my dad would not hear of it. He took the baby from them and decided to raise it as a part of our family. He helped when my aunt was diagnosed with kidney failure. When she needed a transplant, he was the first to volunteer one of his kidneys. His life is complete as long as we are content.

My mother, on the other hand, is more concerned about what others think. My older sister had been going steady with someone for nineteen years and came home one day to tell us that she had converted to Christianity. My mother immediately blamed my sister's partner for the conversion and banned them both from the house. Though my sister had long since moved away from home, I could tell she was hurt by my mother's reaction. My sister confided in me that her decision had not been influenced by her partner. But my mother flew into a rage when I tried to explain this to her then refused to speak to me for days afterwards, and the topic became completely off-limits. I continued to visit with and go out with my sister and her partner. Unlike my mother, I dealt with my feelings. I learnt to be on my own, and avoided being home so that I didn't have to mind my p's and q's around my mother.

Several uneventful years rolled by before I met the person I felt I wanted to share my life with. She had been a regular customer at my work for about two years before I noticed her. She's always been a bit of a plain Jane and I never saw her as someone I could be romantically attracted to. As an introvert, she never really caught anyone's attention. When I did mention her, no one in my office knew who I was talking about. One day, however, I was in complete shock to see that her spectacles were gone, her typical khaki pants were gone and her hair was worn loose. Not a trace of the Pam I remembered remained in the person before me. 'I want to be helped by a person who knows my name,' she said with an attitude so huge that it was more difficult to imagine her as the same person from before.

My colleagues looked at each other, puzzled. No one could recall her name.

Her office had been providing our publishing company with a lot of business over the years, and now it appeared as though an important client had been neglected. She paused a moment to smile at me, then returned her attention to the counter for someone to help her.

'So no one knows my name,' she said, 'yet I've been supporting your business for years,' she cleared her throat. 'That's shocking service,' she headed towards the door.

'Wait,' I interrupted her, 'Pam, I'm Shakirah. How can I help you?'

A smug smile played around her mouth as she told me what she wanted.

'You look different,' I said as I went about helping her.

'I'm going to a party tonight and I won't have time to go home,' she responded. 'I need to get changed at work.'

'So what are you wearing?' I asked.

'A dress, a bit longer than this one,' she answered, 'with the same heels. I'll curl my hair a bit rather than wearing it sleek,' she flashed a beaming smile. 'I want to look different tonight.'

'Well you've succeeded,' I said, still thinking how different she appeared today. 'I must say I'm surprised.'

'Good, it's my intention,' she said taking the parcel from me. 'Would you like to join me tonight?'

I was completely taken aback. I had no idea what to say. I laughed out of embarrassment, and she also giggled.

'Take my cell number,' she said. 'The party starts at seven. Think about it and call me around six or six-thirty. I'd really like you to come and I hope to hear from you later,' she sounded simultaneously confident and nervous as she left.

I was anxious but I couldn't wait to accept. I called her soon afterwards to ask where we would meet and what I should wear.

At the party, she introduced me to everyone as her girlfriend, which surprised me and her friends alike. It seemed that Pam was full of surprises that day. She told her friends about how she'd come to our publishing company only because of me working there. Before tonight, no one had even suspected that she was a lesbian. Later that evening she kissed me passionately. I was reeling in the surprise of the whole evening... and I didn't fight it at all.

I'd never been in a relationship before, so it was a weird sensation to finally have a girlfriend. I was unable to share my joy with my mom. My new girlfriend was a Christian, which made it even harder to break the news. I was eventually forced into telling my mother when we decided to get married a few years later. My mother and younger sister did not welcome the announcement but my dad was happy for me in every respect.

When my sisters came out I vowed that I wouldn't allow my mother to belittle me in the way she had done to them.

I introduced my partner to my father who took to her instantly. 'You both have my blessing,' he said to us, but later admonished my mother for her hardheaded views on homosexuality. 'They need to be who they want to be. They're grown-up and it's up to them to make their own decisions. They will be judged accordingly.'

To celebrate, my father organised a private family luncheon limited to my parents, my sisters, me and our partners. My mother, however, took it upon herself to invite other members of the family, whom my father promptly turned away. He admonished my mother, which infuriated her even more. She got up in a huff and slammed the door behind her.

'Don't worry Dad,' I said, 'we'll make the best of the occasion.'

Between my older sister and me, we served lunch and cleaned the kitchen afterwards then settled for coffee at a nearby café.

The rest of the family went berserk when my parents told them I was lesbian and would marry a Christian girl. I became more determined than ever to prove to the world that being both Muslim and a lesbian was not impossible. My sexual orientation impacted my father most, and the family rejected him as though he was responsible for my 'criminal' behaviour. The strength of my faith and my feelings about Allah became more resolute. I only wish my father did not have to suffer on account of me.

One day, I glimpsed my mother walking down the street with another man, hand-in-hand. I was stunned... couldn't believe my eyes. I rushed home immediately, where I found my father reading the Quran in his room. A pained expression crossed his face as he noticed my expression.

'What's going on, Dad?' I asked.

'*Shakirah*,' he changed his frown to a smile, 'how are you?'

He wrapped his arms around me when I went to the bed to

sit down beside him. I snuggled and lay quietly next to him. The silence in the room helped me formulate what I wanted to say next.

'What's happening, dad?' I asked, and he responded with a baffled expression.

'What do you mean?' he asked.

'You know what I mean,' I said, shifting myself to look in his face. 'Why is mom walking around with another man?'

'Oh,' he sighed and it seemed as if he aged countless in that instant. He heaved a heavy sigh. 'They judge me for allowing you to marry a Christian girl,' he said. 'My sister says she's ashamed to be related to me…. Your mother wants nothing to do with me and threatens to divorce me.'

'So what happened? Did the imam agree?' I asked him, shocked.

'He agreed with me,' Dad replied. 'The imam said he couldn't divorce us because your mother only wants to keep up appearances, and that is not reason enough.'

I loathed my mother in that instant, and decided to confront her when I saw her next.

'Is she still staying here, Dad?' I asked.

'She only shows up now and again. Moena down the street brings food in the evening. I'm at the centre during the day. I'm fine,' he said firmly. 'Don't fret about me when you have yourself and your wife to think about. You don't need an old man hanging around your neck for the rest of your life.'

I laughed at him

'Dad, you'll always be important to me, regardless of who I'm with.' I got up to leave. 'I'll drop in tomorrow evening after work again, okay?'

'Yah, yah…' he replied, reaching for the Quran again. 'Bring Pam with you,' he called as I headed towards the door.

Along the way, I spotted my mother once again. She and that man were kissing on the roadside and she was acting like a silly schoolgirl. Suddenly I realised what it was all about. *She is doing this to get my father to divorce her!* But clearly she didn't know him well enough. Allah himself would need to give my father that instruction. Coming out is difficult and painful for other members of the family too.

Glossary

A

aayaat verses of the Quran

adaab good manners

amien amen, which is a declaration of affirmation; to agree, especially in prayer

Allah Arabic name for God

Allah hu Akbar God is great

As salaamu alaikum peace be with you

Astaghfirullah Allah forgive me

athaan the Muslim call to prayer

B

boeta colloquial for older brother or uncle

bru colloquial for friend

buya Malaysian term for father

C

Day of *Qiyamat* Day of Judgement

deen a term used by Muslims for their religion; way of life

dhikr offering praise in remembrance of the oneness of Allah

duah prayer

F

fajr salaah the early morning prayer that Muslims observe; this is the first of five daily prayers

fitna a trial, but colloquially used to mean gossip

G

gaydar the ability to tell when someone near you is
  homosexual, even if they have given no obvious
  indications of being so; gay internet website
ghusl full ablution (ritual washing) required in Islam for
  various rituals and prayers

H

Hadith a report of the sayings or actions of Muhammad or
  his companions, together with the tradition of its chain of
  transmission; the collective body of these traditions
hafiz modern day Muslims use this word in reference to the
  memorising of the Quran; also means protector
hajj pilgrimage to Mecca as per one of the five pillars of Islam
haraam Arabic word meaning both forbidden and sacred (in
  this case forbidden)
heteronormative a term used to describe the mainstream
  heterosexual marginalisation of people who do not
  conform to the norms set by society, usually in a patriarchal
  system. It also implies that the lifestyles of people that are
  not heterosexual differ from that of mainstream society
  because of their sexual orientation.
hijab the headscarf worn by Muslim women, sometimes
  including a veil that covers the face; also a covering

I

imaan belief, faith
imam Muslim scholar and leader
insha Allah God willing

J

jahannam hell in Islam
jamaah congregation or group
jumuah the Friday congregational prayer
janaazah funeral

janaazah ghusl obligatory funeral bath for the deceased
jannatul firdous highest place in paradise

K
kabr grave
kaffer (Afrikaans) derogatory term used for a dark skinned
   person, usually of African descent; currently it is not an
   acceptable term to use in South Africa
kalimah shahadah a testimony of faith in the Oneness of God
   and the acceptance that the Prophet Muhammad (pbuh) is
   His messenger
kanalah colloquial term for please (derived from Malaysian)
kifaiyat colloquially used to refer to a funeral
koefieyah Muslim prayer cap

M
madressa a school providing education about the Quran, Islam
   and being Muslim
maghrieb formal sunset prayer in Islam
maulana Muslim scholar and leader
Mavis derogatory term for homosexual
meisiekind Afrikaans word for a girl child
moffie derogatory term used for an effeminate man or
   homosexual
musallah prayer mat

N
Nancy no
nogal actually / even

P
PE Port Elizabeth

R

raka'ats units of *salaah* consisting of recitation, standing, bowing and two prostrations

rakam colloquial term used by the Cape Town Muslim community for a framed picture or picture frame

Ramadan the ninth month of the Islamic year, the holy month of fasting, which is one of the five pillars of Islam, ordained by the Quran for all adult Muslims

S

salaam peace; also used as abbreviated greeting form for *as salaam alaikum*

salaah a prayer; a unique institution bringing one closer to Allah by harmonising one's mental attitude with physical posture

shaytan the devil

shebeen local tavern set up from someone's home, or backyard. Some are legal, others not.

shukr thanks

shukran thank you

subhanalla thank God

sujoed a prostrate position on the ground with your forehead, knees, nose and palms of both hands touching the ground

T

tablieghi an Islamic missionary worker

tablieghi jamaat Muslim missionary groups that works towards the revival of the lifestyle of the prophet

tahajud a special prayer done in the latter part of the night made for a specific need

taqwa belief and fear of God

talaaqed divorced

taubah repentance

ta'weez an amulet, often worn around one's neck to ward off evil; also believed to have special healing powers *thobe* an ankle-length garment, usually with long sleeves, similar to a robe

tik another term for crystal meth

touba repentance

U

ulema Muslim religious leaders and scholars who have completed several years of training and study of Islamic sciences/law

umi mother

V

vrymoedigheid Afrikaans word meaning the freedom to do something

W

wudu the ablution that is performed prior to prayer

Y

ya Allah exclamation of surprise

ya nay exclamation

yoh term used for amazement or irritation

Z

ziyaarat to visit (particularly a important place)

More about The Inner Circle

The **Vision** of TIC is:
Transforming society into one of inter-connectedness and inclusivity of different faiths and beliefs around gender and sexual diversity.

The **Mission** of TIC is:
Empowering and raising consciousness around gender and sexual diversity by engaging faith and beliefs; encouraging independent reasoning and collaboration, especially with Muslims who are queer and the local, national and international Muslim community.

TIC **Values** are:
- Leadership (*As-shhura wal Imaamah*): Ensuring accountability, integrity, mutual consultation, respect and being role models and mentors
- Diversity (*Al-Muta'addidah*): Promoting equity, justice and inclusivity
- Patience (*As-Sabr*): Encouraging humility, understanding and nurturing
- Empowerment (*At-Tamakkun*): Imparting knowledge, understanding, skills and developing self-worth
- Authenticity (*Al-Haqeeqiyyah*): Employing honesty, integrity, transparency and trust
- Commitment (*Al-'Ahdah*): Cultivating punctuality, dedication, responsibility, accountability and passion

- Creating safe spaces (*Al-Amnah*): Affirming confidentiality, support, sharing, and respect
- Interconnectedness (*Al-Ukhuwwah wal Ittisaal*): Engaging through compassion, understanding and consciousness

CONTACT DETAILS

Phone: +27 21 761 0037
                +27 21 761 4434

Fax: +27 21 761 3862

Email: info@theinnercircle.org.za

Office: c/o York & Lester Roads
                Witkin Bldg
                Wynberg 7824
                Cape Town
                South Africa

Postal address: P.O. Box 18107
                Wynberg
                7824
                Cape Town
                South Africa

Website: www.theinnercircle.org.za

www.ingramcontent.com/pod-product-compliance
Lightning Source LLC
Chambersburg PA
CBHW072121020426
42334CB00018B/1671